"*Comfort Detox* exposes the way our everyday complacencies keep us from seeing and responding to the needs of those both near and far. With compassion and conviction, Erin Straza shows us how we can and why we must break the habits that serve self rather than others."

Karen Swallow Prior, author of *Booked* and *Fierce Convictions*

"Erin skillfully captures the nature of our addiction to comfort and its power and ubiquity in modern American life. Weaving personal narratives, Scripture, and practical advice, Straza shows how we can leave behind a worldly, desiccated vision of comfort for the true comfort of Christ."

O. Alan Noble, assistant professor of English, Oklahoma Baptist University, editor in chief, *Christ and Pop Culture*

"Our obsessive pursuit of comfort may be the most acute and least diagnosed malady of North American Christianity. In *Comfort Detox*, Erin Straza helps readers imagine something more glorious—if also riskier—than a life insulated from interruption, inconvenience, and even anguish. I am grateful for her invitation to keep company with Jesus—and keep watch with a sorrowing world."

Jen Pollock Michel, award-winning author of *Teach Us to Want* and *Keeping Place*

"In an age when the problems of the world are one keystroke away, never has it been so tempting (or so easy) to retreat into our cocoons of comfort. Never has it been more vital that we don't. In *Comfort Detox*, a simultaneously profound, personal, and practical book, Erin Straza invites us to live for something more than our own comfort—to discover the truer peace that comes from knowing the divine Comforter and extending his comfort to those in need."

Hannah Anderson, author of *Humble Roots* and *Made for More*

ERIN M. STRAZA

comfort
detox

FINDING FREEDOM FROM
HABITS THAT BIND YOU

IVP Books

An imprint of InterVarsity Press
Downers Grove, Illinois

InterVarsity Press
P.O. Box 1400, Downers Grove, IL 60515-1426
ivpress.com
email@ivpress.com

InterVarsity Press® is the book-publishing division of InterVarsity Christian Fellowship/USA®, a movement of students and faculty active on campus at hundreds of universities, colleges, and schools of nursing in the United States of America, and a member movement of the International Fellowship of Evangelical Students. For information about local and regional activities, visit intervarsity.org.

Scripture quotations, unless otherwise noted, are from The Holy Bible, English Standard Version, copyright © 2001 by Crossway Bibles, a division of Good News Publishers. Used by permission. All rights reserved.

While any stories in this book are true, some names and identifying information may have been changed to protect the privacy of individuals.

Cover design: Cindy Kiple
Interior design: Beth McGill
Images: ©Getty Images

ISBN 978-0-8308-4328-2 (print)
ISBN 978-0-8308-8103-1 (digital)

Printed in the United States of America ♾

 As a member of the Green Press Initiative, InterVarsity Press is committed to protecting the environment and to the responsible use of natural resources. To learn more, visit greenpressinitiative.org.

Library of Congress Cataloging-in-Publication Data
Names: Straza, Erin M., 1972- author.
Title: Comfort detox : finding freedom from habits that bind you / Erin M.
  Straza.
Description: Downers Grove : InterVarsity Press, 2017. | Includes
  bibliographical references.
Identifiers: LCCN 2016046159 (print) | LCCN 2016047584 (ebook) | ISBN
  9780830843282 (pbk. : alk. paper) | ISBN 9780830881031 (eBook)
Subjects: LCSH: Habit breaking—Religious aspects—Christianity.
Classification: LCC BV4598.7 .S77 2017 (print) | LCC BV4598.7 (ebook) | DDC
  248.8/62—dc23
LC record available at https://lccn.loc.gov/2016046159

P	21	20	19	18	17	16	15	14	13	12	11	10	9	8	7	6	5	4	3	2	1
Y	34	33	32	31	30	29	28	27	26	25	24	23	22	21	20	19	18	17			

To Mike, the one

who walks with me in this life

and heaps God's comfort on me

every step of the way

Contents

Introduction

Why a Detox?

Detoxing is all the rage these days. A quick online search produces testimonies from people who have detoxed from drugs, alcohol, Diet Coke, toxins, sugar, digital devices, and holiday madness. Programs are available to participate in a spring detox, the Martha's Vineyard Detox Diet, a colon cleanse, a liver cleanse, a full-body cleanse, an emotional detox, a seasonal detox, and even a post-divorce detox.

One thing is sure: we feel the need to remove the things in our lives that are weighing us down and making us feel sluggish. I see comfort as one of these shackles.

In its pure form, comfort is a gift from God. Comfort is even God himself, for he is our Comforter: "I, I am he who comforts you" (Is 51:12). Let me be clear: the comfort of God is not the problem. Like many other things this side of the fall, our understanding and pursuit of comfort is askew. We want comfort, and we can find it in full from God.

The real problem is that we have sought comfort in all the wrong places, everywhere but God. We look for comfort in people, places, and things. We return to the same faulty sources we know because the unknown is scary. We soothe the discomfort of our anxieties with food, shopping, exercise, control, sex, and isolation. Comfort pursuits are endless. We have chased comfort all around, and it has led us to places we would never choose outright. We are all-in, all-out comfort addicts; comfort beckons, and we willingly follow.

A detox is needed if we are ever to experience true comfort that truly satisfies. And so this book is for anyone who is searching for true comfort, no matter your age, status, profession, or background. Whether old or young, rich or poor, male or female—we are all prone to turn to substitute comforts. We all need to learn how to seek the Comforter.

You may wonder whether taking the comfort detox journey will lead you to an ascetic life, one where you must purposefully choose discomfort or pain because that's a more noble pursuit. Or perhaps you wonder whether I will challenge you to live a daredevil life, tackling the things that frighten you the most—skydiving or public speaking or moving to a Third World nation or something.

I assure you, that is not the point of this book. The apostle Paul urges us "to put off your old self, which belongs to your former manner of life and is corrupt through deceitful desires, and to be renewed in the spirit of your minds, and to put on the new self, created after the likeness of God in true righteousness and holiness" (Eph 4:22-24). A comfort detox is this same call—putting off the old ways to make room for the new.

New York Times business writer Charles Duhigg explores the science behind our patterns and routines in his book *The Power of Habit*. Duhigg explains that habits are made up of a three-part loop: a cue (what prompts your brain to autopilot mode), a routine (a pattern that is physical, mental, or emotional in nature), and a reward (the benefit or perk of the routine). Understanding and interrupting that loop is key to breaking a habit.[1] Habits give our brains the ability to conduct regular, repeated functions while in autopilot mode. On the one hand, this gives us more brainpower for other functions; habits are quite useful. On the other hand, our habits make it difficult to switch gears once our cue is triggered. Autopilot kicks in and our habits take over—unless we work to replace them with another habit.

Living for what gives or maintains the greatest amount of personal comfort is our long-established habit. At the core, that's what comfort is—it's a habit, a way of life. Comfort has become the default. We make decisions to protect it without even realizing it. We are on autopilot, and the destination is locked in, returning us to our comfort zone time after time. Duhigg insists that "habits aren't destiny . . . [but] the brain stops fully participating in decision making . . . so unless you deliberately *fight* a habit—unless you find new routines—the pattern will unfold automatically."[2] Freedom is found when undesirable habits are identified and the cue-routine-reward structure is defined, pulled apart, and reframed. In the context of our discussion, the cue is a desire for comfort, the routine is the pattern by which comfort is obtained, and the reward is some form of self-soothing, whether that be control, emotional security, power, status, or the like.

> Living for what gives or maintains the greatest amount of personal comfort is our long-established habit.

Pulling those elements apart is tough work. But really, Christians have an advantage here. New life in Christ infuses us with his Spirit, granting us power to say no to sin and yes to righteousness. With a better understanding of the Spirit's presence and promise to us, we can tackle this comfort habit head on. It will take some prayer, some journaling, some heavenly insight, some time, some practice. We need to introduce new information into our patterns to disrupt our autopilot and wake our brains up from their comfort stupor. Our brains need to engage and make decisions again, instead of floating along the paths of least resistance.

Some habits are so well ingrained that we can't even see them. We've grown blind to them, and our brains are content to run on autopilot. That's another reason why a detox is so beneficial. It will make us aware of the habits running our lives behind the scenes and below the surface.

Awareness is only half the battle though. Once we see how comfort has shrunk our lives down to a fraction of all God intended, then the hard work begins. We have to push back against the mindlessness. We need to practice new habits that are truly life giving, ones that lead us back to God. In a sermon titled "The Expulsive Power of a New Affection," Scottish preacher Thomas Chalmers said, "The only way to dispossess [the heart] of an old affection, is by the expulsive power of a new one."[3] A new affection is the only thing strong enough to overcome an old one. We must become captivated by the God who loves us enough to provide the comfort we so desperately need.

My own comfort detox began with putting off the sluggish and selfish thought-habits I had always practiced. And this is where your comfort detox begins as well: on the inside, dealing with the way you process information to make everyday decisions. I dub this our *decision matrix*. Each one of us has an internal set of values by which we live our lives. When we face a choice, these values tell us—even subconsciously—how a particular opportunity aligns with our value system. The decision matrix runs its split-second analysis, spitting out either a yes or a no, thereby determining our next steps. We each have a decision matrix; the question is, do we know the values that dictate what we agree to and what we decline? It's crucial to know, for this matrix holds much power over us, keeping us within our predefined comfort zones. We will have to take a brave look within to trace words and actions back to the root of comfort addiction. And then we will ask God to do the miraculous: to tear down the old matrix so that he can rebuild a new one set on something more worthy than personal comfort.

Although I am not sure what God will teach you along the way or what he may ask you to do, one thing we can know for certain is that our God is not anti-comfort. Rather, he asks us to put off pseudo comforts to make room for true comfort—the comfort that flows straight from him, our Comforter. We have run for so long to false comforts, however, that true comfort seems hard to find. Running to God is not automatic, even for the Christian. Old habits die hard. So practice we must if we are to develop new ways of thinking about and pursuing true comfort. That's the putting on part that Paul speaks of in his letter to the Ephesians. We need to retrain our brains, our hearts, and our wills to seek a comfort that truly satisfies.

> **We need to retrain our brains, our hearts, and our wills to seek a comfort that truly satisfies.**

This is why we need a detox. Breaking old habits is never easy! And our bad habits have a way of binding us to life-depleting thought patterns and behaviors. Detoxing will upend those draining habits, thereby flooding new life and light into worn-out places. It's an out-with-the-old, in-with-the-new exchange. The detox process is as simple—and as difficult—as that. The Bible tells us that no discipline is pleasant in the moment; on the flip side, however, the hard work of discipline promises to yield a plentiful harvest for those who have been trained by it (Heb 12:11). Saying no to false comfort breaks its hold on our hearts, giving us space enough to breathe, to think, and to seek God and true comfort instead of short-lived substitutes. If we submit to the discipline of saying no to pseudo comforts and saying yes to the real thing, plentiful comfort will be ours to enjoy. Learning to seek God instead of our vices will yield a multitude of blessing. The promised harvest is well worth the detox process.

We must begin by clearing out the clutter and putting off the old ways. Be gentle with yourself as you enter into this process. Ask God to show you how comfort has gone rogue in your life, binding you to unhealthy, ungodly habits. Consider how you can practice saying no to the false and yes to true. In essence, you will be saying yes to more of God's presence and provision for your every need.

To help you keep moving forward in the process, I've included a section at the end of each chapter called Comfort Cleanse. The Comfort Cleanse steps have also been packaged in a free journal available as a downloadable print-ready PDF at ivpress.com/comfortdetox. (A full list of resource links can be found at erinstraza.com/comfort-detox.) Both the book and the journal will walk you through the main concepts of a comfort detox by providing activities and application exercises. Each exercise is tagged as a step, but please know that you may be processing these steps in tandem rather than in succession. Feel free to read the book in full and then complete the Comfort Cleanse steps in weeks to come, or complete the steps as you read each chapter. Either way works.

There is no ideal timeframe for working through the detox, although I suggest reading the book consistently over two or three months so you don't lose momentum. Twenty-one days seems to be the popular standard for breaking or establishing a habit. But research shows it's actually much longer—as short as two months and as long as eight.[4] I land on the longer end of the habit-formation timeline. And maintaining the habits I've introduced and refusing to return to the ones I've put aside? That takes a lifetime. This is a marathon, not a sprint. Just like a sugar detox or a whole-body cleanse, a comfort detox isn't a once-and-done endeavor. What is learned in this season will cause great growth. But as seasons change, I've found myself revisiting old principles and applying them anew to gain new insights and nurture maturity. These ideas keep coming back around.

Of tremendous help in this progressive growth is going the way with others. Living in deep connection to friends who are pursuing Jesus is how we experience that sharpening of character, values, motives, and actions. Left to ourselves, it is easier to return to old habits along the paths of least resistance, leading us right back to comfort's door. Eugene Peterson's comments are helpful: "There are two biblical designations for people of faith that are extremely useful: *disciple* and *pilgrim*. *Disciple* (*mathētēs*) says we are people who spend our lives apprenticed to our master. . . . *Pilgrim* (*parepidēmos*) tells us we are people who spend our lives going someplace, going to God, and whose path for getting there is the way, Jesus Christ."[5] People of faith are disciples and pilgrims, neither of which Peterson refers to in the singular. This is a team effort. We need each other for encouragement, accountability, laughter, support, and company. The people I am on the way with have made this a much better journey.

Most people I know who establish new patterns of healthy living do so in community. What we eat and the activities we choose are greatly influenced by the people we do life with. As we start this comfort detox journey, I recommend that you get your people to go with you. Working together will be easier than if you try to go the way alone. Taking steps together to say no to comfort's lure will give you momentum. We need the fire of others to keep us from growing lukewarm and weary, to remind us why comfort detox is necessary for the health of our souls.

Do you have fellow pilgrims to go the way with? Gather them up. We are going where true comfort satisfies and false comforts no longer hold sway. Invite your people to join the detox. The journey is always made sweeter with friends. In the Comfort Cleanse sections I've included steps you can take together.

We start in part one, "Comfort Gone Rogue," looking at all the ways we live bent on improving our own comfort levels through our own resources. This is where we will face the questions that haunt our hearts and frighten us into hoarding what we have. We will gain insight on how false comfort lures us in and maintains its power over every decision. Daily decisions, relationships, lifestyle choices—all these will receive a thorough assessment to expose hidden pockets of comfort addiction.

Getting our comfort addiction out in the open is a necessary first step in the detox process. We need to know what we're dealing with! After facing our addiction head on, we turn to two beautiful words that divide our journey in half: *But God.* These are the same words echoed throughout Scripture putting an end to what was and signaling the beginning of hope. By working through the detox challenges in part one, we will have mental space and room in our hearts to consider what our lives might be if comfort addiction no longer had the strongest pull on us.

Then we venture on to the middle section, "Comfort Redeemed," where we will find a respite. Here we will pause and rest to consider the beauty and mystery of God's purposes in wiring us to be drawn to comfort. Because we are not self-sufficient, our need for God and things outside of ourselves humbles us. Our need for soothing and help is one reminder, designed to prompt us toward God for the true and lasting comfort we cannot find anywhere else in this world. As we turn from pseudo comforts, our appetites for true Comfort will grow and our satisfaction in God will deepen.

But the detox process doesn't end there! After breaking free from what's false and establishing patterns for what's true, it's time to practice new, life-giving habits. In part three, "Comfort Set Loose," we'll return to those daily decisions, relationships, and lifestyle choices from part one. Here we will live out our calling to be agents of God's comfort and mercy to others, rather than mere consumers and hoarders of it. By practicing these new habits, we will carve out a few new patterns to live by that will change the course of our days.

Getting to the end of a book can be bittersweet. Nothing beats the satisfaction of finishing a good read! But there's also sadness that the journey is done, coupled with uncertainty about how to process and apply new ideas. My desire is to help you finish this read well, so the "Parting Words: A New Kind of Normal" offers encouragement for moving forward in tangible, practical ways. Our new habits will make us into the comfort agents God has called us to be! This is how we can meet a world of need—in our homes, neighborhoods, communities, and world. Once the habits that bind us are broken, we will be free to live fully in the comfort of God.

COMFORT CLEANSE

Step 1: Gathering Your People

Eugene Peterson points out that in the Bible people of faith are referred to as disciples and pilgrims. Neither is in the singular form, which points to the necessity of living in community. The people we spend time with are the ones who hold much sway over how we live day to day. Your comfort detox journey will be much more effective if you go the way with others! I recommend that you:

- Consider downloading the free Comfort Detox Journal. Get the print-ready PDF at ivpress.com/comfortdetox.

- Find a few friends who will commit to the process with you, and write down all of your names.

- Decide how you will read this book and complete the Comfort Cleanse activities; specifically state how many pages or chapters you will read each week.

- Make a plan for discussing what you are learning; it could be a daily text check in, a once-a-week meeting, or a once-a-month gathering.

- Share your desire for taking this comfort detox journey and any concerns you have as you begin.

A Severe Mercy

By the time I stepped off the plane in India, I was spent. Nineteen hours of travel plus the prep frenzy to leave the country had done me in. Our team's 4 a.m. arrival meant my first views of the city were shrouded in darkness; we checked into our hotel rooms to rest a few hours before the day's itinerary kicked in.

If I had known what was ahead of me that morning, I would have stayed in bed. Maybe I wouldn't have gone to India at all.

Up to that point, my life had been rather sheltered. I knew it, but I didn't know the extent of it. I had constructed for myself a comfortable life, one that limited pain of any sort as much as possible. Anything that challenged my comfort was summarily dismissed, avoided, rejected.

But then I went to India, and God shredded my heart. Everything I had come to know went through the grinder and came out the other side in fragmented pieces. This is what I call The Shredding.

It was completely disorienting, to say the least. What I saw and the people I met there broke me—and like Humpty Dumpty, there was no putting this girl back together again. My life will never be the same. I know—it sounds cliché. Girl goes to India; India changes her life. It's not cliché for me, however. It was more than a journey of self-discovery. This was a journey to understanding the very heart of God.

THE SHREDDING

That two-hour rest the morning we arrived was fitful at best. Not the best way to start a ten-day trip through Western India. I was there for my freelance writing work; one of my clients was based in India, providing a permanent, secure family for girls at risk of being trafficked into the sex trade. I was asked to join the organization's staff trip to see firsthand what I had been writing about. I jumped at the chance. Seeing new places is one of my favorite things, and going to India? How exciting! For weeks before, I imagined myself eating curry at every turn, being dazzled by beautiful saris, and meeting the seventy-five amazing girls whose lives had been rescued from destruction. It sounded utterly magical.

In many ways, it was a magical trip. *Surreal* may be a better word. This alternate reality I was dropped into took my own and turned it upside down and inside out.

Complete disorientation should have been listed as the first entry on the trip agenda. After that scant post-flight nap and a bite to eat, our team piled into the vehicles that would take us to one of the red-light districts. The frantic buzz of city traffic seemingly had a life of its own, enveloping our car into its flow. Rules of the road are less formal there, where pedestrians, bicyclists, scooters, rickshaws, and vehicles move fluidly to fill up every inch of road. It was lovely and exhilarating and overly stimulating, especially in my travel-weary state.

As our driver sped us about, weaving in and out of the hubbub, I saw much that looked familiar, reminding me of my version of normal. There were lovely hotels and buildings, shopping centers, fancy restaurants, and luxury vehicles on the streets. The opulence, however, was juxtaposed with something very different from my normal: slum-level poverty. Between newly constructed high-rise buildings were rows upon rows of tarp dividers where a seemingly endless mass of people lived their lives. I strained my neck as we passed, trying to force my mind to make sense of what my eyes were seeing. This was real life for them. This was not normal. At least not for me.

More than 240 million people in India live on less than two dollars a day; another 939 million survive on two to ten dollars a day.[1] Based on what I was seeing, I believed it. My normal, compared to theirs, suddenly looked more like extreme wealth, with all its food, clothing, shelter, sanitation, health care, education, and opportunity.

We drove deep into the city, its crowded, narrow streets packed with vendors selling everything from fresh fruits to sunglasses to fabric to phones. Soon the driver pulled to the side—it was time to get out, to become participants in the bustle.

Our team leader instructed the women to keep sunglasses and scarves on at all times and to stick close. The men were instructed to lead the way and bring up the rear and to keep an eye out for safety concerns (whatever that meant). Then we began walking. I figured we had a bit of a trek, because I assumed the red-light district would be far removed from the regular city life happening around us.

I was wrong. We turned a corner and everything changed. With every step the cacophony of the city faded, replaced by an eerie quiet that seemed odd for mid-morning. There were a few men loitering along the edges of the buildings, staring at us suspiciously. I was equally suspicious, and my heart began to race. *What was this place?* Then it hit me: this was it. This was the district. Just one block off Main Street. Just a block over from the vendors selling food to the people who worked downtown was this place of devastation. Did the vendors and customers know what happened to women and girls just around the corner from where they grabbed lunch or walked to meetings? My mind was racing with the absurdity of this place and its proximity to a regular life that the women and girls in the district would never know.

Walking through the neighborhood, I wanted to both take it all in and shove it all away. Extreme poverty, spiritual heaviness, staring eyes, excited children running around us—all my senses were engaged and my comfort zone was gone.

We visited with several long-time residents of the district. These women had somehow ended up there, either by birth or kidnapping, with no escape save death. Brothel owners and pimps use threats, violence, and abuse to keep their moneymakers in line. City officials turn blind eyes; some even deliver fleeing women back to their captors. There are no gates or locks to keep women inside the district—the system does it instead. The system is a spiritual stronghold, for I could feel its weight from the moment we entered. How could these women survive here, day in, day out? I begged God to help me give each woman respect through my attentive presence, even though I wanted to run. Deep breaths and prayer became my lifeline as thoughts screamed in my head: *How can this be for real? How can this woman survive in such a damp, dungeon-like room? What's that stench? Stop staring! Don't you dare cry.*

Our last visit was with a woman who warmly welcomed us to her one-room home situated in the lower level of a parking garage. The curtain that served as her front door did little to muffle the engine noise or stifle the vehicle fumes just beyond the fabric. She and our team leaders spoke for a few moments in Hindi; it seemed like small talk. It gave me time to look around and see her life. There was a bed, a few shelves with personal items, a chair, a table. But then she wanted all of our attention—she had something to show us. It was her prized possession: a hot plate. *A hot plate.* It allowed her to cook right there in her one-room home. I have never been that excited about my entire kitchen. But I couldn't rejoice over her hot plate because all I could think about was what she faced every night, what she would face later *that* night. I was told men lined up at her curtained door—ten to twenty of them a night. On a good night, those who paid the pimp for sex with her would not beat her. This was her normal, everyday life.

It is estimated that millions of women and girls are enslaved in the sex trade in India alone.[2] The few women I met made this real to me. In light of these women, representative of millions more, my normal wasn't so normal. My normal looked way more like privilege, freedom, and honor. I felt ill over everything I had, everything these women did not. And the thoughts continued to rage at me: *Compared to these women, I can do anything I want with my life. Am I taking advantage of that? What would these women do if they got to live how I live? Am I squandering the life of freedom I've been given? Am I using what I've been given to multiply freedom for others?*

We walked out of the parking garage to the car that would whisk us away, back to the lives we were free to return to. We passed a group of women and children who had gathered to see the outsiders. One woman reached out and ran her hand down my sleeve. I turned and looked into her glassy eyes, giving a weak smile as I kept walking. She looked drugged, lost. What prompted her to reach out to me? What did she want? Whatever it was, I felt helpless. She was stuck in this district life; I would get to walk out and go on with mine. We got into our car, and I closed the door against the brokenness. I was glad to have a window seat so I could stare outside and gulp back tears. The massive ugly cry would have to wait.

THE QUESTION

For the entire drive back to the hotel, all the thoughts inside me could be summed up into one four-word question: *What am I doing?* The Question, as I now call it, screamed at me, inside me, touching on all aspects of how I live and view the world. It was actually the same question that had haunted me on and off over the years.

In the past, The Question had typically come at me in stealth as I went about the daily routine of my typical American life. It pounced most often when I was in an emotionally thin place—running low on rest or high on stress. One minute I would be bustling about, and then I would hear The Question, taunting me for how I was living and whether it mattered at all. *What am I doing?* would echo in my ear, as life would spin on; but it would feel like I had stepped outside time, observing myself detached from a world at full speed. My heartbeat would throb in my ears, my breath would catch, my panic would rise. It makes me shudder just thinking about it.

Have you heard its breathy whisper in your own ear? It isn't pleasant. I hated The Question because of all the discomfort it caused.

I was uncomfortable because I was never quite sure how to answer. For if I had to give an account for myself, on an average day of my fairly average life, this is what I was doing: *I work and I write. I spend time with loved ones. I read and learn. I eat good food. I rest. I entertain myself. I travel. I visit quaint coffee shops and sip four-dollar lattes. I run. I enjoy my home with heat for the cold and cold for the heat; sometimes I even clean it. I attend worship on Sundays. I pray. I play games on my smartphone. I watch TV. I do laundry (unless my husband beats me to it). I make lists of errands. I lose time on the InterWebs.* All these things and more added up to the sum of my life. This was what I was doing. Was this the answer The Question was searching for? I'm still not sure. As I buzzed around, going to work and play, seeking more of the same normal that everyone around me was chasing, I wondered if this was the point of it all. That's why The Question haunted me—because it felt

> **As I buzzed around, going to work and play, seeking more of the same normal that everyone around me was chasing, I wondered if this was the point of it all.**

like something was off, but I was too scared to take a long, hard look at myself to figure it out.

And that's why, over the years, I didn't give much room for The Question to linger: it made me uneasy. It disrupted the comfort I had accumulated, the routines I had established. In response to The Question I had always pressed on in my routines, holding it all tight against my chest and keeping on with the status quo.

That avoidance maneuver ran out of time for me in February 2012 when I went to India.

God's timer was ticking down to the moment when my normal would splinter and crack wide open. Normal could no longer be my shield, my covering, a way of deflecting The Question that sought to pull me into the reality of what I was doing with my life and what the rest of the world does with theirs. With The Shredding, the splintering of my normal, The Question gained full access to my heart.

I had to face it head on.

What exactly did The Shredding do to me? It forced me to see that the point of my life is not me and my whims for gaining and maintaining comfort for personal enjoyment.

It's one thing to hear about the discomfort others experience— extreme poverty, sex trafficking, brothels, slum communities, star- vation, neglect, exploitation, enslavement. It's another thing to see it with your own eyes. Seeing firsthand forces you to deal with reality—to deal with the normal that is not your own. It didn't take even a day in India before I reached total meltdown. The normal I encountered was a punch in the gut.

The magnitude of need I saw was overwhelming. So many women and girls enslaved. So many people living in squalor. So much sickness, hunger, hopelessness, and darkness. There was a world in desperate need of the hope and comfort that only God could provide—yet most of my days were spent gaining and maintaining comfort for myself. This could not be the purpose God had for me. Certainly God had more in mind for me than moving through life in a zombie-like shuffle, dead to the world's needs.

The Shredding affirmed that longing, reminding me that I have indeed been bought with a price for a purpose; my life is not my own. Now that I have been redeemed by Jesus, my life is to be poured out as a drink offering to him. I have the honor of serving as his hands and feet in this world, extending comfort to all who are in need.

If I am to do so, the contrary habits and patterns I've lived by all my life need to be undone. All the ways I've lived to expand my own comfort for my own benefit need to be dismantled. This includes my daily routines, my approach to relationships, and my life pursuits. Each of these areas needs to be examined; the decision matrix I mentioned in the introduction needs to be reset. The Shredding brought an awareness of the way comfort had been ruling my life. Embracing that awareness set my comfort detox in motion.

Your own comfort detox begins as mine did, with a Shredding that will soften your heart to receive all that God has to teach you. Now, my Shredding happened in India, but to be clear, going to India is not the prerequisite for a comfort detox. You do not need to book a trip or do something particularly momentous. God is fully capable of shredding our hearts wherever we are, to help us face the reality that everything revolves around him and his kingdom, not us. The benefits of gaining such an understanding have been invaluable for me, which is what inspired me to craft this book. As you process the ideas and complete the exercises in each chapter, you will be yielding to the heart Shredding needed for your detox and purposefully placing yourself in the pathway of God's life-changing grace. There's a saying that most of life is just about showing up. The principle seems to apply here. Most of the comfort detox process is about showing up in God's presence and growing in awareness that living for personal comfort has dire consequences.

It's also important for me to clarify that India isn't the only place where evil is present. India didn't shred my heart because it is particularly sin ridden and broken. It just happened to be the place for God's appointed Shredding for me. Shadows fall in every country on every continent. Shadows darken hearts and minds of people from every nation and tribe and language. Shadows gather where oppression and injustice of every form rule. There is not a place on earth that isn't plagued by sin and darkness, brokenness and injustice. This is why you do not need to physically go somewhere to experience a Shredding.

But it is true that the shadows closest to us are often so familiar that we no longer see them, and we no longer break under their weight. It takes fresh experiences, surroundings, and inputs for us to see familiar shadows in a new light. You may need to expose yourself to new things so you can see the harsh shadows that linger right in front of you. Perhaps you need to watch a documentary about genocide or serve in a homeless shelter or visit a nursing home or talk to a refugee. Be willing at the start of this process to engage with uncomfortable things. Your willingness to put yourself in the midst of the world's hard reality serves to remove the familiar, the routine, and the comfortable, thereby opening

> **It takes fresh experiences, surroundings, and inputs for us to see familiar shadows in a new light.**

eyes that have grown blind to the shadows. Old things are suddenly seen as they have always been. Stepping outside of our comfort zones forces us to see the reality that's easier to dismiss.

What I saw in India did that for me, raising that vague, haunting Question to deafening levels. It was in India that The Question got in my face and wouldn't let me look away. I had no place to hide. I couldn't busy myself with my normal life and ignore the discrepancies between my version of normal and others'. The normal I had was what I knew, but it was nothing like the normal for the enslaved, the oppressed, the poor, the needy, the outcast, the forgotten. *Normal* became a relative term. I could no longer pretend that everyone lived as I did. Going on with life as usual was no longer an option.

I have come to see The Shredding as God's severe mercy to me. I first heard the phrase *severe mercy* in the book by that title written by Sheldon Vanauken.[3] He writes of the devastating death of his beloved wife and claims that this tragedy was God's severe mercy to draw him to saving faith in Christ. In the same way, going to India and having a meltdown was severe to me, but it was actually God's mercy. This necessary pain made it impossible for all that I was seeing and hearing and feeling in India to be seen and heard and felt *lightly*. Every encounter, every sight, every sound went deep and lodged within.

The Shredding was a painful way—the only way—for me to own what India offered to teach me.

THE CALL TO KEEP WATCH

Once I got home, the pain from The Shredding lingered for months. The awareness I had gained overseas allowed me to see my own community differently. In my small, Midwest town shadows were also near. People struggled with depression and hopelessness, loneliness and doubt, homelessness both physical and emotional. Here the pain can be more easily draped and covered up in well-fed, well-dressed bodies. Pain looked different from the pain I saw in India. But I could no more fix this pain than I could rescue even one woman from the red-light district. My only recourse was to cry out to God and beg him to show me how to move forward. I didn't know how to handle my comfortable life of freedom, health, security, and opportunity. I felt guilty. I felt unworthy. So I sought

my only Refuge, pouring out my tears and confessing my list-
lessness. These cries were not immediately answered, despite my
prayerful demands for relief and direction. But I did sense God's
presence, as if he was willing to sit with me and wait for me to
process everything that was swirling about my heart.

In time it occurred to me that I was shredded after seeing the
smallest fraction of the world's brokenness. I saw only part of the
pain from a few blocks of one city in India. But God has seen it
all—not only what I saw in that one city in that one country, but
the full wreck of every city in every country all around the world.
And in addition to today's pain, he has seen the pain of every day
since the beginning of time for every person who has ever lived. If
I was shredded by one experience, what unbearable grief God must
bear! And if I sought comfort for the portion I saw, if I wanted
company in my sorrows, doesn't it make sense that God too would
long for the comfort of company in his sorrows? When have I ever
kept the Lord company in his grief over this sin-plagued world?

We know Jesus sought the company of his friends before he
went to the cross. The letter to the Hebrew believers says that it
was for the joy set before him that Jesus willingly laid down his life
to conquer the sin that has ruined us (Heb 12:2). Despite the joy,
however, Jesus was certainly bearing the weight of the task ahead
as well as the fear of pain and death. In that great discomfort, he
went with his friends to a quiet garden to seek strength from Father
God. Here's how it's described in Matthew's Gospel:

> Then Jesus went with them to a place called Gethsemane, and
> he said to his disciples, "Sit here, while I go over there and
> pray." And taking with him Peter and the two sons of
> Zebedee, he began to be sorrowful and troubled. Then he said
> to them, "My soul is very sorrowful, even to death; remain
> here, and watch with me." And going a little farther he fell
> on his face and prayed, saying, "My Father, if it be possible,

let this cup pass from me; nevertheless, not as I will, but as you will." And he came to the disciples and found them sleeping. And he said to Peter, "So, could you not watch with me one hour?" (Mt 26:36-40)

In the midst of his grief and pain, Jesus invited his friends to be near, to keep watch with him. They were unable to stay in the pain with him; sleep overtook them that night.

We are now on the other side of the cross; Jesus was perfectly obedient to the Father's redemption plan. Redemption is secured in Christ for us, but until it is fully realized in the age to come, pain and brokenness abound here. Certainly Jesus still looks on us as sheep without a shepherd (Mk 6:34). Certainly Jesus still longs to gather us up like a hen gathers her chicks (Mt 23:37). Certainly Jesus still weeps when we weep (Jn 11:35).

The Man of Sorrows has not changed. He sees every tear, hears every cry, and never ceases to petition the Father on our behalf. "Sit here, while I go over there and pray," Jesus said to the disciples. Could it be that his words apply to us, that he asks us to "remain here, and watch with me"? Our inattention to his grief—our inability to watch with him one hour—is not unlike that of Peter, James, and John. This is what we all want in our grief and pain: the comfort of knowing someone cares enough to enter the grief we feel and be with us in it. This is the fullness of Immanuel, God with us. He came near to be with us in our pain, in our sorrow. And we who have experienced the true comfort of God are to follow in his footsteps, drawing near to those who need someone to keep watch in their worst trials. Only love can propel us to purposefully set aside our own comfort to feel another's pain.

And right there, I found the way forward from The Shredding.

The world, both near and far, is in desperate need for someone to step up and care. It's as simple as that. But it isn't easy. Caring requires something; it costs us. We must spend our comfort to step into the discomfort of others. And who wants to do that? We have lives to lead, work to do, projects to finish, books to read, shows to watch, shopping to do. We don't want to feel the panic of anxiety, the hollowness of grief, the disappointment of betrayal, the fear of need. There's no room for suffering here.

At least, I know I didn't have room for it. I certainly didn't want to feel the mess of emotions—mine or others'—brought on by the brokenness of this world. I had built a cozy, comfy life with a berm about it, keeping the pains of life from getting too close.

But then I went to India, and God shredded my heart so I could feel a fraction of what he feels for us. The Shredding exposed the life I had built as a barrier, the habits I had adopted for maximum comfort. They were keeping me from the very pain and grief that fueled the Lord's passion to go to the cross to free us. By taking me to India, the Lord tore apart this grinch's small heart to grow it back three sizes and more, big enough to take in the reality, the normal that others face each day, both here and abroad.

A. W. Tozer confirms: "The truth is, there are some things you cannot know until you have suffered."[4] Until my heart suffered for the normal that others live, I would not know the answer to The Question with all its fragments and fractures. Without The Shredding, I would have returned home with some travel baubles and mementos, but as essentially the same person. God's severe mercy saved me from a shallow experience in India. It was time, God's appointed time, for me to face the pain of the world.

Because, really, this is the answer to The Question that has haunted me over the years:

What am I doing?

I am working hard to keep the uncomfortable things, the painful things, the scary things, at a safe, comfortable distance.

I have lived in my version of normal, with all of my creature comforts, and I have focused on increasing my own pleasure, safety, and wealth. The buffer I have erected around my life and heart ensures that the pain of the world won't penetrate too far.

Comfort is what I am doing.

Comfort is what we are doing.

Comfort has gone rogue in our hearts. God meant it for something more. Our self-soothing habits are keeping us from experiencing true comfort from God. The scraps we collect from various sources aren't enough, making it all too easy to disengage from those who come asking for consolation in their hour of need. The disciples couldn't stay awake when their friend needed them most; so too are we sleepy in our comfort-rich lives. And so Jesus calls us to engage and draw near to the needs in our midst, to be the sort of friends who draw on the unending comfort of God and eagerly give it away. This is love.

I mentioned previously that God must be heavy with grief over the pains of this world. Jesus was weighed down with sorrow in Gethsemane and asked his friends to keep watch with him. Perhaps there is a way to keep watch with him today—to keep watch with the 7 billion people weighed down with sorrows of their own. Jesus explains how:

> When the Son of Man comes in his glory, . . . the King will say to those on his right, "Come, you who are blessed by my Father, inherit the kingdom prepared for you from the foundation of the world. For I was hungry and you gave me food, I was thirsty and you gave me drink, I was a stranger and you welcomed me, I was naked and you clothed me, I was sick and you visited me, I was in prison and you came to me." Then the righteous will answer him, saying, "Lord, when did we see you hungry and feed you, or thirsty and give you drink?

And when did we see you a stranger and welcome you, or naked and clothe you? And when did we see you sick or in prison and visit you?" And the King will answer them, "Truly, I say to you, as you did it to one of the least of these my brothers, you did it to me."

Then he will say to those on his left, "Depart from me, you cursed, into the eternal fire prepared for the devil and his angels. For I was hungry and you gave me no food, I was thirsty and you gave me no drink, I was a stranger and you did not welcome me, naked and you did not clothe me, sick and in prison and you did not visit me." Then they also will answer, saying, "Lord, when did we see you hungry or thirsty or a stranger or naked or sick or in prison, and did not minister to you?" Then he will answer them, saying, "Truly, I say to you, as you did not do it to one of the least of these, you did not do it to me." And these will go away into eternal punishment, but the righteous into eternal life. (Mt 25:31-46)

Every time we walk in love to extend care to another, Jesus says, it's like we've done the kindness to him. Comfort detox is needed because our habits have been set to self-soothing practices; we've become more like those goats on the left, who turn blind eyes to the hungry, thirsty, lonely, naked, and imprisoned. We've forgotten our calling to be God's hands and feet to a world desperate for someone to keep watch with them. Keeping watch is all about being present, extending care, being attentive. By extending love and comfort to the broken places around us, we keep watch with Jesus in his sorrow.

> By extending love and comfort to the broken places around us, we keep watch with Jesus in his sorrow.

This is yet another lesson from The Shredding: rather than hoarding what I have for my personal benefit, Jesus calls me to give freely to everyone, thereby serving Jesus himself. I can keep watch with Jesus in his sorrow over the sin and suffering in the world by entering into the sorrows of others. I can listen. I can give food and drink. I can cry. I can pray. I can welcome the lonely. I can encourage the downtrodden. I can send a note. I can spend time. I can visit the prisoner. There are countless ways I can do *something* for the least of the world. Small acts of kindness matter, especially to Jesus.

As lovely as that sounds, it sets off a little alarm in my soul. I know myself. My decision matrix has been set for so long on self, it won't be easy to change. Doing so will cost me a measure of comfort—perhaps all I have. Like the disciples, I have fallen asleep on my friend who has asked me to keep watch with him. This is why I need a detox.

Walking through this comfort detox journey will wake us from our slumber. We'll pull up the shades of self-soothing and scatter the shadows of apathy. It's time to venture out of our normal, out of our habits and previously defined comfort zones, and to see what life is like for the rest of the world. It's time to keep the Lord company in his grief over the way sin has ruined us, to let his passion for the world empower us to lay down our lives for the least of these. We must put aside our childish notions of *comfortable* to move on to maturity: to live as God's comfort agents, distributing true comfort anywhere we find a need. We must break the habits propelling us to consume and hoard comfort only for our own benefit. We need God's mercy and grace to detox us—heart, mind, and soul.

COMFORT CLEANSE

Step 2: Embracing Reality

It's one thing to hear about the discomfort others experience. It's another thing to see it with your own eyes. Seeing firsthand forces you to deal with reality—to deal with the normal that is not your own. How can you embrace the reality of the world's normal at the start of your detox journey? Here are a few ideas to consider; pick one of these or create your own to complete in the next week. Visit erinstraza.com/comfort-detox for direct links to all resources.

Learn about one of the following:

- the oppression of women and girls

  suggested resources: Half the Sky Movement (www.halfthesky movement.org); *Born into Brothels*, a 2004 documentary directed by Zana Briski and Ross Kauffman

- systemic poverty

  suggested resources: Compassion International (www.com passion.com/poverty/poverty.htm); *The End of Poverty?*, a 2008 documentary by Philippe Diaz

- genocide

  suggested resources: History.com, "What Is Genocide?" (www .history.com/topics/what-is-genocide); *Hotel Rwanda*, a 2004 film directed by Terry George

- racism

  suggested resources: *Overrated: Are We More in Love with the Idea of Changing the World Than Actually Changing the World?* by Eugene Cho; *Disunity in Christ: Uncovering the Hidden Forces That Keep Us Apart* by Christena Cleveland

Arrange a hands-on experience:

- serve at a homeless shelter
- visit a nursing home
- talk with a refugee
- help a single parent for a few hours

Step 3: A Shredding

Block out thirty minutes when you can be alone without inter-ruption. Ask God to begin shredding your heart for the brokenness of the world. Confess the ways you have avoided facing the reality of brokenness and suffering that sent Jesus to the cross. Ask God to teach you how to keep watch with him for those who are suffering.

PART 1

comfort
gone rogue

Confined

Sometimes I wonder about my life. I lead a small life—well, valuable, but small—and sometimes I wonder, do I do it because I like it, or because I haven't been brave? So much of what I see reminds me of something I read in a book, when shouldn't it be the other way around?

KATHLEEN KELLY IN
YOU'VE GOT MAIL

Oh, Kathleen. You are speaking my language.

Kathleen Kelly is the heroine of the film *You've Got Mail.* She owns an adorable children's bookstore (be still, my heart), which her mother opened when Kathleen was just a girl. When a mega-bookstore opens down the block, Kathleen's store takes a hit financially, forcing her to assess her business and, in essence, her very life. It is in this season that she reflects on where she's been and where she's headed.

Like Kathleen, I also wonder about my life and the smallness of it. I wonder where my bravery has gone, or if I ever had it. I wonder if I've settled, and I wonder why. Such wonderings often arise after I've been sifted by The Question (the *what-am-I-doing* inquiry). When The Question comes, I am jolted, forced to look at the sum of my days and wonder some more.

But deep down I already know the truth: my life is rather small, mostly because I stay where it's comfortable. Kathleen Kelly and I are kindred hearts, mourning over a life that is valuable but lived on the fringes, where bravery isn't needed.

Our everyday choices reveal much about our addiction to comfort. Comfortable habits have led us to a smallness of life akin to Kathleen Kelly's. So this is where our journey begins, in the ordinary, normal things we do in any given moment on any given day.

HOW DID I GET HERE?

No one sets out to live a small life. For proof, think back to your senior year of high school. Before graduation, I bet you answered a survey about your postgraduation plans. My school printed our pictures and dreams in the school paper. There were rows of smiling faces, expectant of a bright future. The answers were varied, of course—and likely off base. I, for instance, said that I wanted to be an accountant. Never mind that I was (am) terrible with numbers and columns and order and such. Obviously I did not know myself very well at age seventeen.

Whatever answers we gave in senior high, we all thought our lives would be fabulous. Meaning, our lives would never resemble those of the adults we knew. Those lives seemed so steady and predictable and responsible and, well, *boring*. No—we would live rousing lives with work that changed the world and values that inspired the masses and passionate love that never waned and endless joy to fill our hearts. Maybe that's a bit dramatic—but the point is no one dreams of living a small life.

Yet here I am twenty-plus years later, a kindred spirit with Kathleen Kelly.

Friends of mine have expressed the same encroaching disenchantment with adulthood. The dreams of our youth did not deliver us from becoming those typical adults with jobs, bills, kids, and responsibilities. We are now the boring ones in the eyes of today's youth. My dear friend Rosa, now in her mid-forties, feels this keenly:

> I have worked at the same company, in the same department, for 17 years. I am very grateful for my colleagues, a wonderful manager, expertise in my field, and favorable compensation. Yet, so many days (that have turned into weeks and months) I am actively disengaged with my job. I wish I had the energy to see what else is out there. But then doubts creep in: *you should just feel grateful to have this job; you probably wouldn't be able to work from home if you switch companies; you are senior level—do you really want to start over somewhere else?* The comfort of the known job outweighs the risks of daring to find something I'm passionate about.

Maybe that's what our younger selves saw in our elders: a settling, an aversion to risk, a willingness to trade passion for comfort. Rosa is not alone. I too have settled into my grown-up life, plagued by guilt for wanting more when what I have is pretty decent. Shouldn't we, especially those of us who have faith in Jesus, be content with what we have? Shouldn't we be grateful rather than seeking more?

If the guilt of contentment doesn't get you, there is the equal but opposite guilt from a sense of duty to live a life worthy of the calling we have received (see Eph 4:1). Whatever a "worthy" life may be, our lives don't seem to measure up to all that. Compared to people who have started grand movements or launched meaningful causes, my life feels less than worthy of the calling. There is a sense, a pressure, that

> **There is a sense, a pressure, that we should *do* something big, and that pressure can squeeze the joy out of walking with Jesus.**

we should *do* something big, and that pressure can squeeze the joy out of walking with Jesus.

These dual guilts of contentment and grandeur take turns buffeting us, tag-team style. I think it's because we really do *want* to live more than a small life. But I for one have had no clue how to do that. My life has taken on a shape, one that I chose sometime after high school—during college, perhaps, or soon after. One decision at a time, I collected the pieces of an adult life.

It's like that life management illustration, the one with the jar (representing your life) filled with rocks and pebbles and sand (representing what you do). You can add any combination of the three elements, but to make everything fit, you must put the biggest (i.e., most important) pieces in first. By the time I reached early adulthood, I had chosen what to include in my life jar (faith, education, career, relationships, interests, and such). Each piece got a bit of testing and trying, Goldilocks style.

Actually, I see quite a bit of Goldilocks in me. I've tried lots of different combinations and permutations to see what would be a good fit for my life. Christopher Booker, in his book *The Seven Basic Plots: Why We Tell Stories*, says the story of Goldilocks characterizes the "dialectical three," where "the first is wrong in one way, the second in another or opposite way, and only the third, in the middle, is just right."[1]

Everyone does this as part of the formation and individuation process. Finding our way forward in life is needful, but stories like *Goldilocks* show the dark side, where we get so focused on arranging our Just Right that we become ravagers, eating all the food, breaking some chairs, and messing up all the beds—leaving a trail of chaos in our wake. This is the Goldilocks mentality.

I know this folly, for I have lived the Goldilocks life on a constant quest for Just Right. Finding my way forward has included plenty of sampling to arrive at the comfy middle ground in things of faith and work and relationships and responsibilities. In time, my choices have added up and given me a very full jar, a full life, with habits and patterns that keep everything in place.

But now? My jar, the inputs, the decision matrix I used to test how it would all go together—all that needs an overhaul. Like Kathleen Kelly, I must gather up some courage and see what sort of life I've been called to lead.

TAKE A RIDE ON THE DISRUPTIVE THINKER BUS

Although I live in the flatlands of Illinois, it's Boulder, Colorado, that has my heart. I've spent extended time there over the past few years, and besides the spectacular views and food, Boulder has a quirky, eclectic vibe, with a strong pedestrian and outdoor lifestyle. There are street musicians and street markets and hippy-like people wandering about. I regularly encounter things that take me by surprise. Including a shuttle bus labeled Disruptive Thinker Transport.

I am smitten with it. The first time I saw it, I almost ran it down to find out what it was for and where it was going. A quick online search told me it was the complimentary shuttle service for employees of international advertising agency Crispen Porter + Bogusky. So very clever. Not only does the name shape the perception of CP+B for those, like me, who see it pass by, but it also must influence how the employees see themselves. These folks are supposed to live up to the disruptive thinker label, people who break out of the expected, the usual, the norm. They take risks, don't conform, and shake things up.

I found myself wishing to be worthy to ride on that bus. Not only did I appreciate the culture CP+B is seeking to develop with these transports, but it also sparked a longing in me to catch a Disruptive Thinker Transport that would deliver me to a new place spiritually speaking. After The Shredding I could see that comfort had a hold of me, but I wasn't quite sure how that had happened.

Nor did I know how to undo what had already become ingrained. I asked God to show me what I needed to know about comfort's hold, and he was faithful to point out the common, everyday habits and patterns contributing to the place where I found myself.

Three high-level strongholds emerged in this evaluation. My decision matrix—the one dictating my choices—was set to keep my comfort zone intact using a protective trifecta: convenience, safety, and perfection. My commitment to these three affected every decision I made, every day. The result? A sort of everyday egomania in which I make everything revolve around myself and my wishes.

Disruptive thoughts are necessary then, inspired by the truth of God's Word and what's real in the world. These strongholds must be assessed and their power broken to set comfort in its proper place. We need to break free from the thought patterns and habits solidifying our commitment to comfort. The Disruptive Thinker Transport can take us, like a bus route, to each of these strongholds. At each stop we see another way comfort's grip has uniquely become part of our daily lives.

FIRST STOP: CONVENIENCE

My jar is full, just the way I arranged it. The rocks, pebbles, and sand are all in there, just right. If my days follow the plan I've concocted, then everything fits—just right.

But life isn't always Just Right. Not typically. Typically, life doles out all manner of unexpected, unscheduled, inconvenient things. And it messes with the Just-Right life that I'm trying to maintain.

My time-blocked and color-coded calendar speaks volumes about my goals and dreams. There's room for God, running, work, writing, meetings, errands, food prepping and eating, and more. There's room for it all, if the way I've packed it is the way my days play out.

Reality is much messier and more unpredictable, however. Reality hands us—and those in our circle—all manner of trouble and discouragement and suffering, none of which I color coded into my schedule. Need does not appear on cue, complete with the tinkling bell alarm, to then disappear on command. When the needs come, I look at my calendar and my commitments and my responsibilities, and more often than not I choose to serve my schedule. Or at the very least I choose whatever option produces the smallest level of inconvenience. *For me.*

That's not quite how Jesus expected his disciples to behave. In one parable, Jesus tells of a man who was attacked by robbers, stripped naked, and beaten (Lk 10:25-37). The hoodlums then left the man for dead on the side of the road. Lucky for the victim, a priest happened to be walking that way; surely someone as good hearted as a priest would stop and care for this man! But no; the priest crossed to the other side of the road, likely pretending not to see him. A Levite came along and responded just like the priest.

I've often wondered where the priest and the Levite were going. Did they have appointments to keep, meetings to attend, ministry commitments to fulfill? Considering their station in life, I'm guessing they had plenty of "good" things to do. Stopping to help a victim would certainly disrupt the schedule and be an inconvenience. They might have had to postpone meetings, extend their time away from home, or miss an event. All inconvenient, to be sure.

As Jesus often did, in this parable he challenged assumptions about who is good and what is important. The story picks up again as the victim's rescuer enters the scene. He's the most unlikely of people, at least from a Jewish perspective: a Samaritan. Samaritans were considered impure, especially when compared to a priest and a Levite. But Jesus chose the Samaritan as the unexpected hero, the only one who did not avoid the man in need. Compassion overcame the Samaritan, overcame the inconvenience it would be for him to stop what he was doing and help. Jesus says the Samaritan man

came to where [the victim] was, and when he saw him, *he had compassion*. He went to him and bound up his wounds, pouring on oil and wine. Then he set him on his own animal and brought him to an inn and took care of him. And the next day he took out two denarii and gave them to the innkeeper, saying, "Take care of him, and whatever more you spend, I will repay you when I come back." (Lk 10:33-35, emphasis mine)

This is how disciples of Jesus are to respond when a need crosses our paths. We are not to avoid the need but to stop and do what we can. Doing so will be disruptive. It will cost us our schedules, our plans, our time, our money—and most of all, our hearts. We will have to engage and feel compassion for the downtrodden. We will have to let the pain of a suffering world shred our hearts, freeing us from the habits we're bound to so that there's room for something greater: compassion.

A. W. Tozer said this in *A Disruptive Faith*: "If need be, God will interrupt your life in any way imaginable without asking your permission."[2] It is God's severe mercy to interrupt us, to inconvenience us, to break us out of our comfort habits so we can extend his hands of mercy to a world in need.

I have a dear—and wise—friend whose logical mind is a huge help to me. But because logic comes naturally to her, Dorothy says the comfort of convenience often traps her:

My natural tendency is to always take the easy way—emotionally, physically, spiritually. When a situation is presented to me, my first thoughts are: *How much time will that take, will it get messy, do I know how to do it?* . . . Convenience isn't necessarily good. It makes you miss out on things, like strong

relationships/friendships, the joy of helping others, closeness
with God, and even the ability to exercise spiritual disciplines.

After hearing my friend's heart, my first thought is that faith is
anything but convenient. It requires much of us—but not without
a return. God will interrupt our lives, but always for good reason—
no, for the best reason. When God interrupts our routines and
schedules, he gives back what Dorothy mentions: strong relationships and friendships, the joy of helping others, closeness with
God, and the fruit that comes from spiritual disciplines.

Going back to the elements of habit outlined by Charles
Duhigg—cue, routine, and reward—I see convenience as a major
reward that motivates me. And as Duhigg explains, the power of
changing a habit is identifying the reward you are seeking and
working backward.[3] Now that I see convenience tagged in my decision matrix, I don't want to live for it.

The cost of choosing convenience as our reward is steep. When
we pass by people beaten up by this life, passed out in the ditch, it's
an opportunity for us to keep watch over them in their suffering.
We have a way to care for Jesus by proxy by caring for the least we
encounter as we go about our day.

To do that, we need God's help. Our habits have us locked into
the same comfort-ruled behavior as the priest and the Levite. We
too have important things to do and places to be. But there is a
greater way to live. When we make decisions based on compassion
instead of comfort, we will emulate the Samaritan Jesus spoke of.

However, convenience isn't the only way comfort fools us into
settling for less than God's best. Let's see how safety plays a part.

SECOND STOP: SAFETY

Something happens to our sense of adventure as we mature. The
recklessness of youth gives way to the reasonableness of adulthood.

Whereas youth are busy gathering and arranging the contents of their life jars, adults are busy protecting theirs. With more to lose, adults enact measures to keep threats at a safe distance. Every action is assessed according to its potential dangers. Don't visit developing countries (illness and disease), don't fly (terrorism), don't switch jobs (financial ruin), don't go sledding (physical harm), don't speak in public (humiliation), don't run alone (abduction), don't eat sprouts from Jimmy John's (salmonella), don't shower during a thunderstorm (electrocution), don't make eye contact with the homeless (guilt), and so on. There really isn't a scenario that cannot be turned into a danger.

At this second stop on the Disruptive Thinker Transport, we need to assess how risk aversion prevents us from responding to the needs before us. This one is tricky. We often lean on common sense in matters concerning personal safety. But what if our common sense has been negatively influenced by our addiction to comfort?

What if our common sense has been negatively influenced by our addiction to comfort?

I sometimes wonder whether that's what happened to the Israelites. God had just led them out of Egypt where they had been enslaved for generations. There were plenty of signs and wonders to confirm God was leading them with power and would protect them. But when they got to the land God had led them to, all his provision wasn't adding up to the confidence they needed to make the next move: "Then the men who had gone up [to survey the land] said, 'We are not able to go up against the people, for they are stronger than we are'" (Num 13:31).

God told the Israelites he was giving them some land. It was a done deal, a sure thing. The spies looked at it, rich with produce and crops. What they saw was good. But before the Israelites could enjoy God's promises, they would have to boot out the current inhabitants—who looked way stronger. In that common-sense assessment, fear took over. The Israelites compared the pros of enjoying the land to the cons of taking it, and the cons shouted much louder. The Israelites said no to the promise because they would have to trade present comfort for future prosperity, and they wanted to play it safe. Tim Challies explains it like this: "Forty years and an entire generation was wasted because fear and a desire for comfort overcame trust in the promises of God. I wonder what opportunities I have wasted already, and what opportunities I will be tempted to waste today, all in the name of comfort."[4] *Ouch.* And so true!

As much as I want to blast the Israelites for failing to move forward in faith, I cannot. I am more like the Israelites than I care to be. It makes my stomach sink just thinking about it. The small life Kathleen Kelly spoke of, the one we lament over, is really about living with small faith. Small faith causes us to wail like the Israelites when God's leading includes difficulty. When faced with risky situations that oppose common sense, how often do we assume God would never call us there? We go into preservation mode—a small life in the hand is worth a large life in the bush. (Or something like that.) Small faith assumes God doesn't have our back. It also assumes that difficulty is always linked to disobedience—because God wouldn't make us work hard or fight for what he's already promised, right?

How many times have I chosen to adhere to the confines of my life jar and the contents therein? How often have I said no to God's prompting to move forward and trust his leading? How often have I chosen instead to stay put because it feels safer to me?

My hesitation is often linked to uncertainty about God's leading. Is God prompting me to start a conversation with a stranger? Is God nudging me to tutor at-risk kids? Am I supposed to turn my car around and go meet the homeless person at the corner? I have said no to all these things (and more). I refuse to move ahead because I am not sure it's safe for me physically, emotionally, or mentally. It feels risky to me, just like taking the Promised Land felt risky to the Israelites.

Common sense tells us to play it safe and do what's most comfortable. But risk isn't as avoidable as we like to presume. Risk is present in any step of faith that places us in a position to be misunderstood, rejected, or attacked. Staying safe has dire consequences, however, that comfort chooses to ignore. The opposite of common sense isn't a daredevil lifestyle, but walking in step with God's Spirit, staying so close to him that we know when to move, when to speak, when to stay silent.

Living for safety in the middle of what's comfortable isn't the sort of life God calls his people to. The main goal isn't safety and comfort, but God's fame and glory. I doubt God's fame is increased and his glory uplifted when I live tucked inside my comfort zone, fearful of venturing outside its protective borders. Small faith like that diminishes God's reputation. Small faith like that doesn't extend God's comfort to people desperate for hope.

God has more for us. Following God's lead will mean leaving our previously defined comfort zones behind. If we stay in step with God, we will live and move and have our being in the middle of an endless safety zone that cannot be taken from us. That's where we are meant to live, there in the middle of God's will, where we move forward into seemingly unsafe places emotionally, physically, and spiritually. And there we find that God has our back.

THIRD STOP: PERFECTION

Somewhere along the way, I got the idea that people who have it all together (whatever that means) experience life like a choreographed dance. A waltz perhaps. Or those lovely English country dances featured in *Pride and Prejudice*. Everything is spinning and turning in proper time and place, with nothing out of order. It's the picture of perfect coordination.

I thought that if I had my life jar packed just so, I would know how to make my life spin like a beautiful dance. Everything would fall into perfect place. Like magic.

Something has been out of whack though, because my life isn't quite like a fancy waltz—maybe more of a mosh pit. Everything gets jumbled and crazy, and I find myself swept off my feet, unable to steady myself.

When life doesn't move according to Elizabethan propriety, I blame myself. I wonder if I need dance lessons. I assume I've made the dance too complicated for my level of coordination, that there are simply too many moving parts. I assume a perfect life is out there to be had, if only I could figure out the steps.

At our final stop on the Disruptive Thinker Transport, we need to look at how we strive for a flawless, perfect life. Our obsession with it drives our daily choices, and not for the better.

My tendency has been to say no to anything that could intensify the mosh pit. How could I add something else to my already-crazy life? I'm aiming for *Pride and Prejudice* here. Getting involved with someone else's needs and wants will only increase the spinning and make it more difficult for me to keep up. Saying yes depletes my comfort, requiring me to give up order and ease. Comfort convinces me that the cost of keeping watch in someone else's hour of need is too great. If I'm going to maintain my beautifully coordinated, Just-Right life, I cannot take on another thing.

Women especially struggle with the pressure to have a picture-perfect life. Pinterest, Facebook, and the church all show us what's expected. Martha Stewart's craftiness. Ree Drummond's culinary prowess. Jillian Michaels's fitness. Mari Kondo's home organization. Joanna Gaines's home décor. And

do it all with the zen of Oprah, the tireless faith of Christine
Caine, the wisdom of Priscilla Shirer, and the compassion of
Katie Davis Majors.

Such effortless perfection actually takes concentrated effort.
There's research, serving, leading, cooking, achieving, and praying
to do. There's no space for others in this dance toward perfection.
Once again, the Shredding has exposed my comfort-driven
thinking: If I craft a perfectly ordered life that's beautiful to
observe but keeps people out, is that the sort of life God wants
for me?

Making my life a perfectly crafted performance drives me to
keep up the illusion that I can do it all and handle it all with ease.
Fixing my eyes on that prize pushes me to eliminate all other dis-
tractions, including the very people God has called me to keep
watch with. While I'm busy concocting a life for others to gush
over, I don't have time or energy to have the deep connections my
heart craves. I've got it all wrong when I seek comfort from the
perfect life I create with my own hands.

Joy is found in the connections, with people and work and pas-
sions and service. Every time I eliminate a connection because it
feels like too much effort, I'm cutting off life. I hack at my commitments at church, potential friendships, visiting the sick, treating
my nieces and nephews, hosting a benefit event for my favorite
nonprofit, scheduling coffee with my mom, spending time with my
husband, tutoring a kid in need—and on and on.

When we are driven to choose whatever maintains the illusion
of perfection, we stay in the middle of comfort—stuck in a rut.
Once again, this false comfort has fooled us. We have traded true
life for a sham. Like those buildings on movie sets, it looks real, but
there's no substance. The result is something that looks pretty from
afar, but there's no life in it. It's a lifeless life.

And what's the point of that?

Lifeless life is the very thing Jesus came to rescue us from. Jesus promised, "I came that they may have life and have it abundantly" (Jn 10:10).

False comfort whispers that we should turn back from the abundant life God promises because it's full of things that cannot be controlled and crafted—and that's rather uncomfortable. Striving to maintain perfect order causes us to waste all that Jesus has secured in his life, through his death, and be-

> **Lifeless life is the very thing Jesus came to rescue us from.**

cause of his resurrection. We have at our disposal the resurrection life of Jesus Christ to help us live for more than that! What Jesus has secured makes it possible for us stop striving for a perfectly ordered life, because he wants to live his perfect life through us— meaning we can step into the chaos of this world and keep watch with people who need something real.

GIVING UP MY JUST-RIGHT LIFE

I have lived a small life, on the fringes, where bravery isn't needed. I have heard the groans of the world, and I have turned a blind eye and a deaf ear because it wasn't easy, it looked risky, and it would upset my rhythm. I have pursued comfort with great gusto, only to find that it has overtaken me. This is common variety, everyday egomania, in which I live to make life all about me. And I want it to remain comfortable, safe, and perfectly ordered.

We live lives of small faith trying to stay pain-free and happy. It's the false notion that I can keep the borders of my life secure, guarded against any attacks from the enemy named discomfort. My comfort zone needs to be small enough for me to patrol and protect. There isn't energy enough to protect too much territory— I have rounds to make, people! I have to keep watch in the night. I have to run interference by holding an arm out against life itself, trying to keep it from getting too close.

At least, that's what I thought before The Shredding. The Disruptive Thinker Transport did its job, however, forcing me to look at all the ways I try to arrange my Just-Right life. Convenience, safety, perfection—these are daily habits built choice by choice, and they will have to be undone the same way, choice by choice. Breaking old habits and building new—that takes time, as well as lots of grace. More than that, it takes a change of heart.

Living for convenience, safety, and perfection are easy faults to admit. It's like confessing the general sin of worry. Similar to worry, however, these three indicate something more serious lurking below the surface. They serve as a dashboard reading for the heart's ability to engage fully with others. Our habit structures are in place for an important purpose: to protect us from the pain that will diminish our personal happiness. So our everyday choices do more than make our days run smoothly; they also keep our hearts from getting too involved with others. It's time to move on to deeper waters, to see why we choose to live so detached and numbed out. Our hearts have much to tell us.

COMFORT CLEANSE

Step 4: Detoxing from Convenience

Pick a day this week to disrupt your cue-routine-reward habit loop for convenience. In the morning, ask God to alert you to how you are insisting that life adhere to your plan. Whenever inconveniences pop up, embrace them and ask God to help you say no to self instead. Write down what happened and what you learned.

Step 5: Detoxing from Safety

Visit erinstraza.com/comfort-detox and follow the link to take the Risk-Taking Test from PsychTests.com. Process your results by working through the following questions:

- As you answered the questions, did you discover anything new about how willing you are to embrace risk?

- Based on the quiz questions, does it seem that your risk aversion is masked as common sense?

- How does having your decision matrix set to safety cause you to dismiss opportunities God may be calling you to embrace?

Ask God to show you where you have become content to stay encamped in the wilderness rather than moving forward in faith to the Promised Land. Is it a relationship? A job? A character flaw? A step of faith? How can you choose to live for more than safety in this area of your life?

Step 6: Detoxing from Perfection

Amy Carroll, author of the book *Breaking Up with Perfect*, has an insightful interview about cutting perfectionistic ties. Visit erinstraza.com/comfort-detox and follow the link to listen to the interview.

Process the power perfection has on you by working through these questions:

- When is the lure of perfection the strongest for you?

- What appeals to you about having a life that others envy?

- What do you lose by trying to project a perfect life?

Identify the main area in which perfection is ruling you. Ask God to help you say goodbye to perfectionistic thinking in that area this week, and write down what happens.

- 3 -

Detached

*To love means to open ourselves to suffering. Shall
we shut our doors to love, then, and be "safe"?*

ELISABETH ELLIOT

The pain-averse part of me wants to answer Elisabeth
Elliot's question in the affirmative: *Yes! Let's be safe. Let's avoid
suffering and all its pain and sorrow and grief and fear and unknown.*

Even so, my heart yearns for love, putting me in a constant tug-
of-war with love on one side and safety on the other. I have felt
this battle for as long as I can remember. I want to give and receive
love, yet I long to be emotionally safe. My decision matrix is forced
to work overtime, trying to balance out these dueling desires and
keep me in my comfort zone.

It's a lot of work, and then The Question comes knocking. I'm
caught off-guard, and I see my folly anew: love—true love—will
never be comfortable in the way I hope. It is inherently risky. Love
requires the suffering of self-sacrifice, just as Elliot mentions. Love
calls us into scary territory, where there are no emotional guar-
antees. Love requires us to feel all the feels.

Fear of feeling too much has pushed me to shut the doors of my
heart, posting No Trespassing signs along every stretch of its perimeter.

There are friendships I've neglected, conversations I've avoided, intimacy I've sacrificed, help I've refused to give, and more, all because I am scared to feel too much. And I know I'm not alone, because fear was the most common reaction I got after I shared what I experienced in India. Eyes would widen, full of emotion, after learning of the people I saw in the red-light district or the tarp communities. Comments would vary, but few people wanted to delve deeper by knowing more. Comfort zone alerts were squawking inside their brains, telling them to shut down that informational burden ASAP.

Emotional safety is a powerful component of comfort addiction. We've adopted patterns and methods to limit our emotional risk. But those very habits promoting emotional distance keep us from experiencing the love we so desperately long for and the love we are meant to give away. As scary as it may be to embrace the depth of feeling we're capable of, this is the necessary next step in our comfort detox journey. Let's dig into detox stage two.

> **Those very habits promoting emotional distance keep us from experiencing the love we so desperately long for and the love we are meant to give away.**

AN EVER-SHRINKING CONCEPT OF LOVE

If I close my eyes, in a flash I'm back in sixth grade. It's a March morning in 1984. A frigid winter wind has just pushed me to my first day at a new school. As a Navy family, we had logged at least seven moves during my childhood. It's fewer than many Navy families, yet change was part of our family DNA.

On this day, at eleven years old, I did not yet see the positives of these frequent life disruptions. But I did know the new-girl-at-a-new-school drill: *Go with my parents and meet the principal. Listen to the adults agree that everything will be wonderful. Walk in dread*

toward the inevitable with my parents and the principal to the new
classroom. Meet the teacher in the hallway as the students stare at and
whisper about the new girl.

I don't remember exactly what the grown-ups discussed, perhaps
because I was too anxiety ridden. Questions like these were
churning up my heart and stomach: *But who will sit with me at*
lunch? What will I do at recess when everyone runs off with friends?
Who will bother to talk to the new girl?

Previous moves had taught me that new friendships were risky,
starting with gusto and fizzling out when the winds of childhood
preferences shifted. Sadly, girls often rally around common en-
emies. New girls with short histories were easy exclusion targets
for whichever girl ruled the roost. *Mean Girls* rings true for a reason.
I can still hear one girl hiss at me: "We don't want you here! Go
back to wherever you came from!" She pronounced that in the
lunch line, her posse behind her, likely too scared to go against her
proclamation. And I can remember another time of panic and
stinging tears upon finding an insensitive rejection note from girls
who had decided the new girl was no longer welcome to their
group. Such brutish behavior taught me to proceed with great
caution in forming new friendships: first, because I had suffered
from them in the past, and second, because our move rate meant
long-term friendships weren't likely anyhow.

All these experiences shaped my first-day feelings that March
morning. I survived, of course. And I actually completed my sec-
ondary school education in that same system—six years straight
with the same students. But sadly, I never fully attached to them.
The relational fear I embraced in childhood proved difficult to dismantle just because time passed and the scenery didn't and I grew
older. It carried on into college, into my young adult life, even into
my marriage. My habit was to stay on the fringes with most people,
aloof and scared of being ostracized and rejected. I had long ago

shut the doors of my heart to be safe from whatever might steal away the emotional comfort I so desperately wanted.

Many life lessons come to us in the haunted moments of our earliest days, when we have neither the wisdom nor the capacity to process them. When we are most vulnerable—when we are young and scared or grieving or disappointed—we let these lessons in and give them access to our hearts. Like emotional squatters, they take up residence and give us a way of living, making choices, and assessing situations. This is how we learned to live life only half-heartedly, only partially engaged. Somewhere way back when we experienced heartache and discovered a pain we'd rather not repeat.

Childhood losses are cruel, first cuts that tell us the harsh truth: this world is not all good and right. Maybe the loss for you was a favorite toy—the one that listened to your secrets and provided company in the dark. Maybe the loss was a place of honor with a friend—the one who used to choose you started to choose someone else instead. Maybe the loss was a loved one—the one person who seemed invincible proved to be only human after all. Into all these losses false comfort speaks a lesson to us, offering a way through life that might bypass more pain.

Most of us have learned some version of this lesson. With each passing day we adhere to it, repeating it, wearing the path to full-fledged habit. By the time we are old enough or wise enough to consider the lesson's message and impact, the rules have become second nature. We are comfortable with our means of emotional comfort.

What is it we have learned? We have learned to live—but *just barely*. We live half-lives, settling out on the fringes of events and situations. We live on the periphery where we can't be too affected by pain and discomfort. Just as false comfort shrinks our everyday lives down to minuscule proportions (as we saw in chapter two), it also shrinks our concept of love. Our hearts get locked up in this tiny prison, put on rations, and made to survive on emotional scraps. It's like twenty-three hours in lockdown with just one hour of exercise in the yard. What heart can thrive on that? We were made for more. But comfort has lured us into this prison and convinced us we should be locked in for our own emotional safety. Comfort tells us our primary goal in life is to be emotionally secure, to avoid the discomfort of feeling too deeply or risking a painful experience. The truly sad part? There are no guards to force us to submit. There are no locks keeping us inside the confines of our emotional safety zone.

Oh, but there are chains. We put those on ourselves. We bind ourselves to relational rules that squelch intimacy with others. *Don't overshare. Don't get too attached. Don't pry. Don't be needy. Don't show weakness. Don't be a burden. Don't risk getting involved.* I have lived by these rules, sometimes aware of it, other times not. We distance ourselves from situations or people that challenge these rules.

This is why we want those in pain to keep it in check. We want brutal honesty with a heavy dose of reserve. *Don't come to Bible study a mess and sidetrack the group. Don't unload the truth of your heartache in the aisles of the local grocery.* There are social cues to keep, and we should all be mindful to do so. Paul David Tripp explains it like this in his book *A Quest for More*: "It's not just that we all tend to build our own little claustrophobic kingdoms, but that we want the people who are around us to keep the rules of our kingdoms as well."[1]

We expect people to pick up on the unspoken rules about personal sharing. We have rules because that's how we feel safe. Without the guardrails in place, we fear, the brokenness of others will get too close and compromise the security of our kingdom. Once you practice these rules long enough, they become full-fledged habits.

This may be why no one else notices my heart's retreat from potentially painful situations, but I see it, especially now after The

Shredding. When I was in India I saw some of the worst things people are made to endure in this life: abject poverty, human trafficking, homelessness, orphanhood, corruption, and more. These are things I knew about before my trip, but my fringe living allowed me to be informed yet detached. (I believe this is what Jesus dubbed "lukewarm"; Rev 3:16.)

I had it all wrong. If love requires risk, I would actually have to break all those relational rules I had adopted. The Shredding did that—breaking apart old habits and old ways, clearing the way for my heart to love in all its glorious risk.

HAVE PAIN, WILL HIDE

Fringe living isn't new. It is, in fact, an automatic response. This is home base for us, where we run for emotional cover when our fears get stirred. The pattern began with the world's first encounter with pain, when human hearts first bent under the weight of sin, back in the Garden of Eden.

Within the pristine beauty of the Garden, man and woman were naked and unashamed—they had nothing to hide from each other or from God. They knew God intimately; he walked through the Garden, seeking their company. Everything was working the way it was supposed to, in perfect harmony. What would that have been like? Imagine knowing God so intimately that you never wondered whether he cared or whether he was really listening or whether he was actually angry with you. Imagine being so connected with your loved ones that you not only hid nothing, but you truly had nothing to hide. Imagine knowing exactly who you are and what you were created for, with no lingering doubts or fears or concerns for the future.[2]

This is the picture of perfect peace, of shalom. That's what Adam and Eve had at the time of the creation. There was no reason for Adam and Eve to live on the fringes. They had no reason to shut the doors of their hearts—at least, not yet.

We don't know how long this shalom lasted, whether it was a day, a year, a decade; the Bible gives it just two chapters. Then Adam and Eve chose to trade in shalom for the promise of something more. Autonomy sounded good, so they reached out for the forbidden fruit—and got bondage with the first bite. Their sinful choice immediately disconnected them from God; shalom evaporated. No longer were Adam and Eve intimately related to the Creator, the source of all, the One who is love.

Overwhelmed, they did the only thing they could think to do. They hid: "And they heard the sound of the LORD God walking in the garden in the cool of the day, and the man and his wife hid themselves from the presence of the LORD God among the trees of the garden" (Gen 3:8).

We too know the absence of shalom, the tenuousness of emotional security. We've chosen forbidden fruit, and we're affected when others choose it and their choices blob over onto us. Fear looms over us like the groundhog's shadow, causing us to run and hide in our burrows with eyes squeezed shut to the darkness.

I totally get that. When I'm scared, I detach and disconnect from God and others, hiding my heart, trying to protect myself. I hide because it hurts.

I see a homeless man with a sign, begging for food and money, and I avert my gaze or change my route. I hide.

I overreact to a decision I don't like, growing frustrated with people who think differently from me, and I pull back from the relationship out of pride. I hide.

I hear a friend's words laced with frustration toward her husband, and I don't want to expend the energy to get involved, so I change the subject or offer an empty platitude. I hide.

I see images of starving children in Africa, of slum communities in India, or of mass violence in the United States, and I detach from the reality and move along with my day. I hide.

Here in the shadows I see others who are hiding too. We tuck ourselves among the trees to avoid the grittiness of life, to keep far from the shadow of the fall. Like Adam and Eve, we do this not because we are heartless, but because we fear our hearts will break under the tidal wave of pain that threatens to crash upon us when we face reality. And that, my friends, is why detaching seems like such a good option.

SPIRITUAL MORPHINE

Information about the world's suffering swamps our senses. There isn't time to sort and process. There is only time to breathe before the next wave hits. Since the passing of Garden shalom, our hearts have tried to stay afloat in this world flooded by suffering. Pain, tragedy, disaster, betrayal, death, sickness, loss—it becomes too common, too regular, too much. Shutting it down, pushing it away, and diminishing its impact are our means of survival. It's not that it isn't horrible. It is. But the horror *just doesn't stop*. No heart can run ramped up like that every minute of every day.

Out of necessity, most of us scan recent news and happenings, making mental notes of which pieces we will give our hearts to or bother thinking about for more than a few seconds. Which means some pieces—even some weighty, serious, meaningful ones—we must discard and push aside, for our frames were simply not designed to carry the burdens of the entire world. We must find a way to detach so our hearts do not explode from all the emotional turmoil.

Our anesthesia of choice? A little something called *acedia*. It's an ancient religious term that has come in and out of use over the centuries. I first heard of it after picking up Kathleen Norris's book titled *Acedia and Me*, in which she covers the origins and history of acedia, describing how at its core it is a sort of filter through which we engage the world: "At its Greek root, the word *acedia* means the absence of care. The person afflicted by acedia refuses to care or is incapable of doing so. When life becomes too challenging and engagement with others too demanding, acedia offers a kind of spiritual morphine: you know the pain is there, yet can't rouse yourself to give a damn."[3]

Spiritual morphine—that's one powerful metaphor. Morphine is meant to deaden the pain of trauma within the body; acedia is the spiritual equivalent, deadening the pain of trauma within the heart. And like morphine, acedia is highly addictive. When emotional pain threatens, comfort addicts turn to acedia for a hit. It works by buffering the world's happenings through a cloud of disconnect. Comfort tells me that I cannot possibly extend care for every dark shadow caused by the fall; therefore I should just step back, detach, move along. Acedia eventually saps the heart's ability to do the work it was designed to do: to feel. Our hearts are emotional muscles, requiring regular use for optimum functioning. Acedia prevents proper feeling, however, and in time emotional atrophy sets in.

Norris reports that monks referred to acedia as the "noonday demon" that steals away passion and care for the work at hand.[4] It strikes after a length of caring and engagement, after our reserves are tapped. Noon is the

> **Our hearts are emotional muscles, requiring regular use for optimum functioning.**

midway point, the hinge of the day—there are just as many hours of work ahead as behind. With energy sapped, the monks had to press on in their work despite acedia's lure to shut down the heart and coast through the afternoon on emotional fumes.

Acedia may attack literally at midday, but it isn't necessarily tied to the clock. Any time we feel weary from life is when acedia comes calling. It tells us to go the comfortable route, to detach and reserve our emotional energy for ourselves. Acedia tells us we've cared enough.

It sounds good, reasonable even. We take another hit and let the fog blind us to the peril. Acedia works because it hurts to love others and care about the shadows they live in. False comfort offers plenty of reasons for staying detached and numb, for keeping a safe minimum distance from the suffering.

In my own detox journey, I discovered two lines of thought that were reinforcing my addiction, enticing me to stay numbed out on the fringes: my need to fix things and my desire to keep a comfort stash.

A SAVIOR COMPLEX

Acedia made a dramatic showing one ordinary summer day in Boulder. My husband, Mike, and I were walking to the farmers market, chatting about nothing in particular and enjoying each other's company. Our route to the market could go through the Pearl Street Mall or around it. Same distance, just different scenery. As we discussed our options, I made a comment that came seemingly out of nowhere. I said I'd rather not go through the Mall as there was too much "oddness in there."

You see, the Mall is full of people hoping to gain some cash through begging or a street performance. Some are artists or students; many are homeless and desperate for help. You can't go far in Boulder without being reminded that shalom has been broken. But that day I wanted to pick and choose my encounters with brokenness. With my admission, the ruse was up and my aversion exposed: I wanted to alter our route so I could avoid people who were obviously needy.

Despite the ugliness of my heart, my husband was gracious; we both knew it was a true but not-so-shining moment for me. We continued with our plans and enjoyed a lovely day together, but at the edges I was discouraged. I couldn't shake the painful truth: there were acedia-ruled places in me that needed to be confessed and rooted out.

After that, Pearl Street Mall represented all I have tried so hard to sleep through in this life: homelessness, despair, poverty, hunger, desperation, fear, need. God was gently reminding me that the point of my life is not to preserve my own comfort. He has redeemed me to be his hands and feet, his agent of comfort who will extend grace and mercy to others and keep watch with all who suffer. Pearl Street Mall became my Nineveh, the place I first avoided but was unable to quit. I was drawn there day after day as I asked God to break acedia's hold over my heart. It became like some sort of spiritual showdown, like challenging the noonday demon to pistols at dawn.

On one of my walks through the Mall, I wasn't twenty feet in before a weary-looking young man shuffled by with a dirty backpack and sign at his side. I looked him in the eye and greeted him with a weak "Good morning" and an even weaker smile. As I passed, he sputtered spitefully, "I hope *your* friend doesn't die today!" My heart's comfort alarm began to squawk, but I chose to turn back, to understand why he would say something so harsh.

I asked him to explain. He said he had just learned that a friend in Florida didn't wake up that morning; she had died in her sleep. He needed money to attend her funeral. I asked more questions, about his friend, his name, his pain. Even though I stopped and gave my time and ear and attention, this man would not have wanted my heart, for it was full of rotten thoughts like these: *Was he telling the truth? Did a friend really die? Was this his sob story to gain my sympathies and some cash? How long do I need to listen before it's okay to move on? Do I have to give him money? What if he just wants drugs or alcohol?*

The reality is his story could have been a scam—desperate situations push people to desperate measures. But behind these common-sense arguments, beyond the suspicions and doubts that were raging, I could hear something else: acedia's voice urging me not to let my heart care, to remain aloof, frozen, asleep, *careless*.

On this day, in this situation, I chose to ignore acedia. Once I chose to care, something miraculous happened: my heart surged to life. I was immediately overcome with compassion for this young man and the loss he was feeling. I too have known heartache. I too have known darkness and pain and hopelessness. In my own moments of grief, the presence of Jesus has made all the difference. *Did he know Jesus? Did he have any inkling that Jesus loved him, died for him, longed for him to be restored to the Father?*

Offering this man Jesus was the best I had, so I asked him if I could pray. He agreed, so I gave voice to the parts of my heart that were now teeming with life and actually feeling my feelings, and I lifted it all to the throne of grace. Prayer placed the two of us on level ground, equal footing before God. Our needs were different, but we were both desperately needy. We were the same at heart.

Acedia's fog often dulls this reality, blurring our ability to see not only the neediness of others but also our own. And to be honest, we don't really want to know the extent of our own need. So we post the signs and bolt the doors and take another dose of acedia to keep the obviously needy people out so we can ignore the truth: we are actually one of them.

My prayer did not deliver travel money to this man's feet. It did not stop his tears. It did not bring his friend back from the grave. It did not solve his homeless situation. It did not usher in repentant faith in Jesus (at least not that I know of). I wanted all of that for him. I wanted him to have a shower and clean clothes. I wanted him to know that Jesus was near to the brokenhearted and loved him beyond measure. I wanted him to have hope, joy, and purpose. That's what happens when your heart starts to engage: you want everything to be set right.

A heart that is awake sees the awful effects of the fall and rails against them. That is a tender place to be, though, because in this world there will be trouble and the poor will always be with us.

It isn't all fixable. I hate that I can't fix it, which makes my heart hurt all the more.

If pain cannot be fully eradicated, if poverty cannot be completely resolved, if all the captives cannot be freed, if the oppression cannot be entirely lifted, then what's the point of doing anything? Why should I awaken my heart to feel the pain caused by things that cannot be resolved?

This hopeless summation is one of the greatest reasons acedia has appealed to me. But social researcher Brené Brown counters, "Numbing vulnerability also dulls our experiences of love, joy, belonging, creativity, and empathy. We can't selectively numb emotion. Numb the dark and you numb the light."[5] My lifelong habit of pushing away the pain that can't be fully resolved wasn't completely without merit. It likely prevented some discomfort. But it definitely limited my ability to engage with others. Detaching from pain detached me from love, since there is no love without pain, no joy without suffering. As Elisabeth Elliot said, to love is to suffer. My loss far outweighed the gain.

SCARCITY MENTALITY

My encounter with the homeless man forced me to face my fear, my pride, my inability to help, my own need for the comfort that only God can supply.

It is true that I lack the resources to undo all the pain that sin has wrought in this world. I don't even have the resources to undo all the pain that sin has wrought in me. It took a Messiah to break the power of sin, and even so we are waiting for the day when all will be fully restored. Until then, we live in the already/not yet, this place of limbo where we walk by faith, not by sight.

But the things I see, even through the eyes of faith, break my heart. We are in want for more of God's power and promises in our daily living, especially in places of emotional unrest. Even Jesus wept when death stole away his friend Lazarus; he cried despite knowing that in mere moments Lazarus would be breathing again. The pain and suffering of this world cause us to weep as well, even though we know God has promised to restore life in full one day.

But today, in this moment? Sin's shadows darken our lives. And the darkness hurts. This is why shutting the doors of my heart can sound like a good option. In this already/not yet era, I evaluate my encounters with others in terms of what it will cost because I want to hang on to as much comfort as possible. This is what addicts do—they aren't willing to share because they want to keep all they have for themselves.

Brené Brown explains that "scarcity thrives in a culture where everyone is hyperaware of lack."[6] When resources are lacking, we react by pulling in and shutting down to conserve what we have. Engagement is justified only when resources are plentiful and not otherwise in use or earmarked for other purposes. Scarcity mentality measures out life by the ounce; it always concludes that the needs outweigh the resources. When the shadows gather, I fear my reserves won't see me through. I choose to extend care based on how little it will deplete my reserves. Most of the time, acedia tells me it's better to stay aloof and uninvolved, to keep what I have to meet my own needs. Acedia tells me to conserve my comfort, to save it up—because what I have isn't enough and I am not certain God will come through with reinforcements.

> **Scarcity mentality measures out life by the ounce; it always concludes that the needs outweigh the resources.**

Some needs in life truly are draining. Some people are exceptionally needy. We have to gear up for such encounters and then recharge afterward. How do we push against scarcity mentality in situations that consistently zap us of resources? Every one of us struggles with similar relational concerns: *Are my boundaries healthy, or are they merely a way to play it safe?* Unhealthy people and relationships are real and require real wisdom, and oftentimes real distance. Let me stress that such cases *are situational and circumstantial.* And this is not acedia.

Acedia is more of an approach to life: *it is universal and habitual.* It tells us to pull back from caring about anyone or anything because we simply cannot spare the effort. Generally speaking, acedia is at work when we choose not to care because we are counting on our own resources instead of the endless supply that comes from God alone.

What acedia fails to tell us is that even if we detach, even if we spare the resources, *there still won't be enough.* When we pull away and hoard our comfort stash, it dwindles and eventually runs dry. We will always be in low supply; there will never be enough in stock to justify sharing it.

Jesus taught his friends a lesson about sharing scant resources when a crowd of thousands grew hungry and there was no food to give. The disciples wanted to send the people home, but Jesus urged his friends to gather whatever food they could find. One boy in the crowd had a meager snack of five loaves and two fish. When the disciples began asking who had brought food, this boy did not hold back, even though offering it would not feed a crowd of thousands. Wouldn't it have been better for him to keep it for himself if it wasn't going to help anyhow?

We don't know why the boy gave his food to the disciples or what he was thinking. But he gave what he had to Jesus, refusing to hoard it. Jesus took this food that would scarcely satisfy a child, and he multiplied it to feed thousands.

Sadly, my comfort addiction prompts me to keep what little I have for myself. What if I would willingly, trustingly give what little I have to Jesus? He would turn my scarcity into abundance, feeding many, including me. My detachment and selfish hoarding leaves me—and thousands of others—hungry. It robs us all of the miracle that Jesus would perform to meet our needs and satisfy the hunger of our souls.

When we hoard comfort for ourselves, we live in a state of self-inflicted scarcity, for Jesus is our never-ending Source. Comfort addiction fools us into depending on our scant reserves when we have the riches of God available in Jesus. In him we find everything we need, and his mercies start fresh every morning.

But we don't believe it. We believe God is withholding from us. What we believe about God is powerful; it affects every aspect of how we live. My friend Kerwin knows this firsthand. He went through a troublesome stretch in which he became overly de-manding—of God, his wife, his children, and everyone else. When others did not meet his expectations, anger and control rose up. In time God showed Kerwin the source of his trouble:

> I did not see God as an abundant father eager to give to his children. My prayers were like a Christmas gift list: Here's what I'd like, but I probably won't get most of it. Just the socks and underwear. I believed the Lord put me on the "minimum wage" blessing list (which is this scarcity mentality). I be-lieved he'd only give me enough to keep me in the faith but nothing more.

What we believe about God's provision for us in the moment makes all the difference in how we live in the moment. If we be-lieve God won't abundantly give us everything we need for life and godliness in Jesus, then we will live in fear of want. We will demand, as Kerwin did, that others make up for what we perceive as a lack from God. We will hoard and grow angry when we don't have what we want.

Scarcity mentality tells me it's too risky to love others. When my heart is numbed to others it is also numbed to Jesus, which prevents me from drawing on his infinite resources. My finite resources tell me to control the outcome, to push people away, to conserve, to shut the doors of my heart and refuse to engage. Only with Jesus as my supply will I venture to open my heart to the world. When he is enough, I don't have to be.

WE CANNOT STAY HERE

Any place where we are living detached and disengaged is a place in desperate need of God's comfort. He is calling out to his children, "Where are you?" He calls to each of us in love, urging us to come out from the fringes and shake our hearts to life once again. Only his love can clear acedia's numbing fog from the landscape of the heart.

Brené Brown explains that "our willingness to own and engage with our vulnerability determines the depth of our courage and the clarity of our purpose; the level to which we protect ourselves from being vulnerable is a measure of our fear and disconnection."[7] Operating out of fear and disconnection is a half-life at best. All our comfort habits flow from a fear of being vulnerable, a fear of engaging, a fear of feeling. If we're going to break free from our comfort habits, we must put off our savior complex and scarcity mentality.

Band of Brothers is an award-winning HBO miniseries following a company of US soldiers serving in World War II. In one episode, the company is instructed to run from the forest covering through an open field to take over a key town in France. The company lieutenant (who has long proved his inability to lead) and about half of the men make it midway across the field to a large haystack before gunfire pins them down. Fear grips the lieutenant, and he insists they stay behind the haystack for protection. Gunfire begins ripping through the hay and bombs begin exploding around them. The soldiers demand a plan, knowing they face certain death by waiting in that field. One soldier gets in the lieutenant's face, yelling, "We cannot stay here!" Fear, urgency, and frustration collide, making this scene one of the most vivid of the series.[8]

And it applies well to our comfort detox journey. Fear may be screaming for us to sit tight and hide from this fight for freedom. But that soldier is right—we cannot stay here. We cannot keep on practicing comfort habits of detachment because we think we need to save the day or hoard our resources. Doing so leaves us numbed out and detached from love, just as C. S. Lewis explains in *The Four Loves*:

> Love anything, and your heart will certainly be wrung and possibly be broken. If you want to make sure of keeping it intact, you must give your heart to no one, not even to an animal. Wrap it carefully round with hobbies and little luxuries; avoid all entanglements; lock it up safe in the casket or coffin of your selfishness. But in that casket—safe, dark, motionless, airless—it will change. It will not be broken; it will become unbreakable, impenetrable, irredeemable.[9]

Staying put is a sure death. We need to move forward, putting off the habits that are numbing us from love. But love is more than a feeling. Love works itself out into our actions and behaviors—our very lives. You can tell much about what a person loves by looking at how they invest their lives and use their resources. We need to take this comfort detox journey a bit deeper still, to see what dreams have captured our hearts and what habits are ruling our life goals. And unless our hearts are functioning properly, our life pursuits will be greatly hindered. Although it's scary to feel these emotions, being scared is better than being numb. It means the heart is doing what it was designed to do: feel all the feels.

COMFORT CLEANSE

Step 7: Detoxing from Acedia

Spiritual apathy causes us to simply not care about others. In relation to comfort addiction, acedia is the way we detach so that we do not have to get our hearts involved in the trials of others.

- When are you most tempted to play it safe with your heart and refuse to love?
- When are you most tempted to disengage from the pain of others and the world?

Step 8: Detoxing from the Savior Complex

The weight of the world stirs in us the desire to set things right. But when the needs outweigh our abilities, we pull away and detach. Our need to save others actually prevents us from giving what we can: our care.

- How bad is your savior complex? Visit erinstraza.com/comfort-detox and follow the link to take the savior complex quiz from *Revival Magazine*.
- What are you learning from evaluating your own savior complex?
- Ask God to show you how the savior complex is affecting your relationships.

Step 9: Detoxing from Scarcity Mentality

Comfort addiction fools us into depending on our scant reserves when we have the riches of God available in Jesus. Scarcity mentality prompts us to hoard what we have instead of freely giving to those in need.

Ask God to show you hidden pockets of scarcity mentality that are ruling your thoughts and decisions as you process these questions:

- When are you most tempted to recoil from the needs of others because you feel deficient?
- Why is it difficult for you to trust God to meet your needs?
- How does scarcity mentality affect your everyday decisions and relationships?

- 4 -

Absorbed

But even in the much-publicized rebellion of the young against the materialism of the affluent society, the consumer mentality is too often still intact: the standards of behavior are still those of kind and quantity, the security sought is still the security of numbers, and the chief motive is still the consumer's anxiety that he is missing out on what is "in."

WENDELL BERRY, *THE ART OF THE COMMONPLACE: THE AGRARIAN ESSAYS*

Of the many discussions I've had with people about comfort addiction, most inevitably land in what Wendell Berry calls the consumer mentality. While comfort in the form of emotional distance (chapter three) or everyday egomania (chapter two) may be easier to hide, comfort in the form of lifestyle choices is rather obvious. Identifying the materialistic among us is easy enough. It's always someone whose lifestyle is more expansive than our own. At least that's what I've always thought. Which may be why I once fancied myself part of the youthful rebellion Berry speaks of. The standard I had raised to measure materialism placed me well under the judgment bar.

Still, the *what am I doing* Question prodded me over the years, inquiring about actions and motives I had excused in myself.

Consumer mentality was alive and well in me, lurking beneath the surface of my life pursuits.

Awareness (and admission) of my consumer mentality was yet another result of The Shredding. The living conditions I saw in India reframed my previous definition of a normal life. I was forced to acknowledge the truth about my normal and the sort of life I was able to live. In light of that truth, I could see materialism as an iceberg of Majority World society: the tip you see is nothing compared to the girth below the surface. Even the rebellious youth who aren't obviously materialistic are yet driven by an unseen force to seek comfort through consumption and maintaining the illusion of relevancy. None of us is immune.

Why are we so driven to consume and achieve? I think it's because egomania and emotional numbness cannot provide the sort of lasting comfort we crave. When they don't satisfy, but comfort addiction encourages us to feast on the opportunities before us to have, be, get, and pursue more. And here in the United States? There is always more to be had. Our society produces new ways to be "in" every day.

The painful truth is that I have been way too consumed by the consuming I do. That sort of addiction busies me with tending to the unholy trinity of me, myself, and I. That's why in this third detox stage we need to put down our self-made measuring sticks. Becoming aware of the motives and values lurking below the surface is necessary if we are to find the true comfort our hearts crave.

THE DREAMER IN ALL OF US

The invitation was a surprise. A couple Mike and I knew only casually invited us over for a visit. Because it was one of the first social invites we had received after getting married, it felt significant. I tried to muster all the maturity I could from my insecure, recently married, twenty-year-old self.

Upon arriving we were welcomed into a cozy family room with overstuffed couches, where a few others were already seated. Greetings were extended. Refreshments were offered. And then a more formal introduction began for a man seated near a paper flip board. That's when I realized the evening had some sort of agenda. In a flash I concocted a whole theory: *Maybe they are Christians! We will get to bond over shared faith! They are going to share the gospel!*

Icebreaker-like questions ensued. "What are your favorite things to do, outside of work? If you could travel anywhere, where would you go? Do you like to collect things? What do you like to buy when you have extra money to spend? What sort of car do you dream about owning?" It was easy, energetic conversation. It felt a bit like making a Christmas list, something I had not done in years. Sharing these preferences was fun, and to be honest, my heart was all in. I was starting to dream about things and experiences. I figured that after we shared our answers the discussion would transition to finding true meaning and purpose through Jesus Christ.

I cannot explain my disappointment when the discussion leader promised that all our dreams were indeed possible. Not because Jesus had something greater for us, but because this guy was extending an exclusive invitation for us to get in on the ground level of an exciting and fast-growing business opportunity (AKA multilevel marketing). This was not about the gospel.

We did not accept the exclusive invitation that night. Looking back, I'm amused by my naive evangelism theory. But something else has stuck with me that isn't as amusing: my ability to join the chorus of voices proclaiming all the stuff I want.

Wanting things is not inherently wrong. Giving voice to our preferences is not wrong. Dreaming about what could be is not wrong. The bothersome part is how easy it was to conflate worldly based dreams with gospel hope. How could icebreaker questions about hopes and dreams lead to either the best news humanity has ever heard *or* the opportunity to join an MLM team?

Part of that answer lies in the very foundation of our society. At the birth of the United States, the founding fathers constructed a framework for our country's values and pursuits. The Declaration of Independence states, "We hold these truths to be self-evident, that all men are created equal, that they are endowed by their Creator with certain unalienable Rights, that among these are Life, Liberty and the pursuit of Happiness."[1]

The pursuit of happiness is part and parcel to being an American. Comfortable living has been all but promised, since being unhappy is anything but comfortable. For centuries now people have equated the United States with the place where dreams come true. It's where you are free to work hard, increase your wealth, and enjoy the good life. We call it the American dream.

The phrase "the American dream" was first used in James Truslow Adams's 1931 book, *The Epic of America*. Adams says it's "that dream of a land in which life should be better and richer and fuller for every man, with opportunity for each according to his ability or achievement."[2] Part of what makes the United States unique is the freedom—theoretically open to every individual—to obtain a better, richer, fuller life.

More than eighty years later, talk of the American dream is still going strong (especially during election season). Although definitions vary by person, a core component of the American dream is wealth, as confirmed by a September 2015 article in *The Atlantic* titled "Who Still Believes in the American Dream?" A reporter traveled the country asking people to share what the American dream meant to them. When kids were asked, they gushed about future happiness rooted in fame, glory, and fortune. The adults responded with much less enthusiasm. Many were discouraged by the lack of opportunity they had for achieving their dreams; few were hopeful for the life Adams described back in the 1930s.[3]

Since the American dream has always been connected with prosperity, we have tied our happiness to our ability to collect material possessions and immaterial opportunities. It's no wonder people are disillusioned and discouraged.

ALL IS VANITY

Despite the broken promises of the American dream, our society still runs on that founding premise. We adhere to its values of working hard and striving for more. We do this by participating in the agreed-on system: work, play, eat, sleep. Get a better job. Get a better house. Get better clothes. Get better gadgets. Then repeat. And repeat, and repeat again. The system tells us happiness increases as our creature comforts grow. Pseudo comforts beckon us to seek more of what we already have, because more is always better.

It takes a strong soul to stop the madness and call the futile cycle to the carpet. That's exactly what Solomon did almost three thousand years ago. As

> **The system tells us happiness increases as our creature comforts grow.**

the son of the most accomplished king on record, Solomon had everything—wealth, intelligence, and people. But the book of Ecclesiastes records the comfort his heart longed for:

> Smoke, nothing but smoke. . . .
>   There's nothing to anything—it's all smoke.
> What's there to show for a lifetime of work,
>   a lifetime of working your fingers to the bone?
> One generation goes its way, the next one arrives,
>   but nothing changes. . . .
> There's nothing new on this earth.

Year after year it's the same old thing. . . .
Nobody remembers what happened yesterday.
And the things that will happen tomorrow?
Nobody'll remember them either.
Don't count on being remembered. (Eccles 1:2-11
The Message)

Every time I read these words my chest tightens a bit. Solomon's hopelessness is so complete, so brutal. All our attempts to achieve something meaningful result in nothing substantial. We gain no ground. The comfort we seek in life—at least, the kind that's easy to get—is fleeting at best.

Eugene Peterson's rendition of Solomon's lament uses the phrase "Smoke, nothing but smoke" to signify the evanescent nature of life's pursuits. Traditional Bible versions have, "Vanity of vanities! All is vanity"—which I prefer, actually. *Vanity* has a weight of loss connected to it. A note in the ESV Bible explains, "The Hebrew term *hebel*, translated *vanity* or *vain*, refers concretely to a 'mist,' 'vapor,' or 'mere breath,' and metaphorically to something that is fleeting or elusive."[4] Vanity is what our hearts can sense when everything we are pursuing and consuming in life leaves us empty. Vanity is the fear that pounces when we are bored, unsure of what we should be doing with ourselves. The Question tries to jolt us out of vain pursuits, out of the consumerist cycle that leaves us empty despite all the filling.

Although Solomon wasn't an American, his lament is fitting for those of us caught in the American dream today. We work hard to gain more. We follow our tired routines every single day. We look for amusement to stave off boredom. We seek power, status, riches, and accomplishments to quiet The Question, for if it lingers, we will face the same despair as Solomon: life is nothing but vanity.

But face this truth we must, if we are to rebel against the false comforts that have been on the prowl for centuries. The ones that Solomon denounced are the same ones we must denounce today.

VAIN MEASURES

Prosperity isn't necessarily a bad thing—it's what Jesus promised to give us: "I came that they may have life and have it abundantly" (Jn 10:10). The difference, however, between the prosperity Jesus offers and the one that's foundational to US society is *the way in which that prosperity comes.* Jesus says abundant life—the kind that lasts—can only be found in him. Our society focuses on just one sort of prosperity, the external kind brought on by consuming, owning, and obtaining things.

Sadly, the church has adopted these same faulty measures of happiness, wealth, and comfort. Christians have sanitized it, of course, but it's still the American dream at its core. In the Christian version, material wealth (goods, disposable income, etc.) is seen as God's stamp of approval on our lives and actions. Immaterial wealth (talents, prestige, opportunities, etc.) is seen as confirmation of God's need for us to do something big for the kingdom. In sum, this is the prosperity gospel, where health and wealth are earned and deserved and blessing is bestowed because of personal right-eousness. Never mind that plenty of deserving people suffer and plenty of undeserving people prosper.

The truth is that God blesses because he is good, not because we are. "For [God] makes his sun rise on the evil and on the good, and sends rain on the just and on the unjust" (Mt 5:45).

When our theology flows out of our cultural values, the result is a quasi-Christianity that looks only slightly different from the rest of US society. Hidden under the shiny veneer of faith we have the same consumer mentality, the same standards of behavior, the same need for security, and the same motives to have the latest and greatest. We don't notice anything amiss because our lives fall in step with the faithful around us. A. W. Tozer explains it like this in *The Pursuit of God*: "We have accepted one another's notions, copied one another's lives, and made one another's experiences the model for our own. Now we have reached a low place of sand and burnt wire grass and, worst of all, we have made the Word of Truth conform to our experience and accepted this low plane as the very pasture of the blessed."⁵ This low plane becomes the foundation for life pursuits and goals tied more closely to the American dream than to the abundant life. Egocentrism and acedia birth within the comfort addict the pursuit of a lifestyle set to expand personal happiness through the accumulation of more wealth—even as we turn blind eyes on the least that we've been called to keep watch with.

I am familiar with this low, dusty, burned-out land. Lots of little things keep me shackled to the American dream instead of yoked to abundant life in Jesus. Previously I mentioned how I had once fancied myself as part of the youthful rebellion against materialism. I never thought of myself as driven by things because the typical pursuits don't come easy to me. Fashion has always befuddled me; shopping stresses me out. I forget to run errands so I don't have as many opportunities to be in stores to spend money. And I'm terrible at decorating. Based on this assessment, I thought I was off the hook.

But after The Shredding I became aware of the part comfort played in my lifestyle. For example, when the seasons change, pseudo comfort plays on my fear of being out of fashion. I assess my wardrobe, pronounce it lacking, and go about searching for "the essentials." (Somehow I never have these, even though I often justify my purchases as such.) All it takes is a quick visit to my favorite online shops, and in minutes I've curated the need-to-have items. It's so quick and easy, I hardly count it as shopping.

But it's not just clothing—I entertain and pursue the ideals of the American dream after I visit a lovely home (my house always needs something else), walk into a bookstore (I want all the books, all the time), or hear about a better job opportunity (more status or money would allow for more whatever). Pursuing more sounds good because I always want to increase my comfort. It's easy to grab a new something-something and experience a small surge of joy.

Don't think I'm saying that all material things should be eschewed or that every possession should be sold to give money to the poor (Jesus' correction to that sort of severe asceticism is recorded in John 12:1-8). No, material things that provide momentary pleasure and joy are not evil—it always comes back to the weight and place of them within the heart. The abundant life Jesus spoke of isn't opposed to the material, but it consists of more than *just* the material. Discovering the difference is the point of this third detox stage.

> **The abundant life Jesus spoke of isn't opposed to the material, but it consists of more than *just* the material.**

THE REAL 1 PERCENT

A few years before The Shredding, God began shaking my foundation of comfort. The sands began to shift as I read Richard Stearns's book *The Hole in Our Gospel*. Stearns is the president of World Vision, an international compassion organization that provides food and economic partnering opportunities to those in abject poverty. What I read sent me into a heavy sorrow. There are millions of children—even now, at this very moment—who are orphaned and living alone because both parents died of sickness or genocide. Entire communities are, at this moment, displaced and wandering, searching for food and a new place to call home. Story after story brought the world's version of normal to my awareness. Tears were at the ready for weeks after I took in this reality.

One comparison that Stearns offers rattled me. He uses the analogy of keeping up with the Joneses, that proverbial family with the 2.3 kids, a home in the suburbs with a two-car garage, a picket fence, and a dog.[6] The Joneses also have steady work, access to health care, extra money for some luxury goods and entertainment, plenty of clothes, and a car or two. This typical family has dependable income to make life comfortable. As I read about the Joneses, I felt like I knew them. These are the regular Americans we all know. We would count the Joneses as normal, but certainly not wealthy.

Stearns argues otherwise. Research shows that the US Joneses aren't so typical when compared to the rest of the world. The Joneses are, in fact, some of the world's wealthiest people:

- 93 percent of the world's people do not own a car.

- 3 billion people live on less than $2 per day.

- If you make more than $25,000 per year, you are wealthier than 90 percent of the world's population.

- Only 1 percent of the world makes $50,000 or more per year.[7]

Did you catch that last statistic? We hear much about the "1 percent" in the news; they are scorned as the wealthy elite. They are always someone other than us, of course. But to the rest of the world? Our middle class Jones family could be featured on VH1's *The Fabulous Life Of* or CNBC's *Secret Lives of the Super Rich*. Most people around the world have no means or ability to keep up with the Joneses.

The trouble isn't that the US Joneses are making $50,000 a year. *The sad part is that they don't consider themselves wealthy.* Comfort has fooled us all into comparing ourselves to one another in our closed circles. We huddle together, wishing we had more of this, that, and the other, never realizing we are in the wealthy minority of the world. An article in *The Atlantic* titled "Why Americans All Believe They Are Middle Class" expounds: "From Real Housewives to pop stars, extreme wealth is on display all around us. Seeing this, Americans imbibe ideas of what life as a rich person means. And most folks, even in the 1 percent (that is, with incomes above about $500,000), can't keep up with the Kardashians. They conclude they are not wealthy."[8]

If we do not feel wealthy when we view the lives of the rich and famous, what must the world think when they see the typical American life from their perspective? Our efforts to keep up with the common standard may be subtle or hidden or even subconscious. It may be the way of the land. But the way we view our status affects everything else, including our life pursuits.

Generally speaking, we concentrate more on arranging more for ourselves than we do on sharing our wealth with the 99 percent of the world that has far less. If we see ourselves as middle class at best, then we assume the wealthy are the ones with the extra money; we assume the wealthy are responsible for sharing their extra with the poor. And since we don't see ourselves as wealthy, we've let ourselves off the hook. We go back to arranging and striving and collecting as usual. Comfort wins, soothing us back into our gathering and hoarding practices.

Despite our regular attempts to gain an ounce more of happiness through greater material things, the pursuit hasn't delivered on its promises. The law of diminishing returns tells us that adding more comfort to the stash won't produce a significant increase in satisfaction. But we play the odds and give it a go. We want to prove the rule true for ourselves, at least. So we shop at stores, through catalogs, and on the Internet. We eat gourmet food and throw out the extras. We upgrade and renew. We remodel and renovate and add on. We declutter to make room for more. It's an ongoing and never-ending pursuit of more and bigger and better.

Don't get me wrong: I've found much of the pursuit to be fun. But that fun tends to suck me in deeper than I meant to be, like a riptide hauling me out to sea. I'm pulled along with everyone else. I'm so busy seeing what others are buying and doing, I hardly notice how far from shore I am. That's what consumerism does to us—it traps us and amuses us so that we don't even notice how far we've drifted. Compared to the people around us, we're normal, doing normal things.

We desperately need to see ourselves from the world's perspective.

AMUSING OURSELVES TO DEATH

The best recent depiction I've seen of this blindingly inward focus was in the movie *The Hunger Games*, based on the dystopian novel by Susan Collins. In the book and subsequent movie, heroine Katniss Everdeen lives in District 12 of the nation Panem. Life in the twelve districts is harsh; each one produces a specialized resource to support the ruling class that lives in luxury in the Capitol. To keep the districts in line, the Capitol holds an annual Hunger Games, a televised fight to the death in which two youths from each of the twelve districts are chosen at random to compete. Katniss is forced to the limelight when she volunteers to take her younger sister's place in the Games. Her journey takes her to the Capitol, where fashion, food, and socializing are the tasks of the day. Clothing and makeup are gaudy and overdone. Homes are the height of luxury. The food that was scarce in the districts is so plentiful in the Capitol that partygoers ingest an elixir to purge their full stomachs just so they can keep eating. It's gluttony to the extreme.

My first reaction when I saw the Capitol as depicted in the film was to think, *That's me. That's what I'm doing here. I'm looking for fancier clothes, more jewelry, more home decor items, more luxury—and all the while, the rest of the world would like some bread or proper shoes or the ability to read. I am the real-life Capitol.*

The disgust I felt may have just been magnified by powerful storytelling and great cinematography. But my reaction is affirmed by the statistics compiled by Richard Stearns. We are generally clueless about the harshness of life for the majority of the world. Cluelessness is the grout holding this mosaic together. It allows us to continue on, "amusing ourselves to death," as author Neil Postman opined in his book of the same title.

When money abounds, opportunities for distraction are plentiful. The opportunities opened by material blessing do not come without cost, however. I think of a phrase uttered by Zophar, one of Job's dreadful counselors. As Job mourned the loss of his family and scraped his oozing sores with pottery shards, Zophar attempted to speak wisdom into the situation. From his perspective, Job was suffering because he had sinned; if Job would simply get his life right, his suffering would cease. God later debunked that bit of crazy from Zophar, but within his message was this little gem of a phrase: "In the fullness of his plenty he will be cramped" (Job 20:22 NASB). Fullness does this to the best of us: when we have plenty of everything we could ever want or need, it eventually turns on us. Fullness cramps us, binding us to a certain sort of lifestyle.

This is why my heart grieves. For most of us who live in the United States, we have enjoyed a fullness that has bound us to a certain lifestyle. I can be quite busy about my business of maximizing comfort for myself, easily forgetting that most of the world would count themselves rich if they only had my leftover scraps.

Before The Shredding I was completely unaware that I was bound up by the plenty I enjoy. Sure, I would have said my life was good, that I had access to some creature comforts, but I would not have counted them extreme. I've seen TV shows like *My Super Sweet 16*, *The Housewives of [Whatever-City]*, and *Keeping Up with the Kardashians*. I'm not living *that* sort of life.

But the level of comfort we enjoy in the United States is dramatically high compared to the rest of the world. We live in it, breathe its air, soak in its warmth. It shapes how we think, how we move, how we choose what to do each day. We are so very accustomed to comfort, we hardly notice its presence. But it is always there, permeating everything we do and following us everywhere we go. We may be most aware of its presence when our comfort levels are threatened or challenged.

To be honest, I don't think about pursuing comfort because I don't have to pursue it—it's already here, owning my every moment. But when I'm confronted with a decision that infringes on my comfort, it becomes painfully clear how committed I am to protecting it.

VAIN GOALS

Despite what I've learned about my status as part of the 1 percent, it's still difficult to grasp when everyone around me lives similarly. Most of the time I don't feel rich, which may be why I'm so easily wooed by comfort's offers for material soothing.

But the lifestyle of soothing is more than just material in nature. Wealth enables me to make my life a custom-made self-improvement project, whether it is my health (physical pursuits), my intellect (mental and emotional pursuits), or my soul (spiritual pursuits). Give me a new book, a new idea, a new process, a new course to take, a new locale to explore, and I'm there. It sounds interesting and fun, and I want to do it all.

The time and effort required to tackle all this personal greatness is extraordinary. It takes a lot of time and concentration to make your own life fabulous. With so many amusements available, there simply isn't time or energy left to think about the rest of the world.

Why do I cringe when I see someone hurting, in need of support? Why do I avoid scary activities that have an element of risk? Why do I post signs on my heart telling people to stay away?

I respond like this because I am worried about how it will affect me above all else. Anyone who has read the Gospels knows this doesn't line up. Jesus calls us to "love others as well as you love yourself" (Mt 22:39 *The Message*). Considering my propensity to live small and stay numb to maintain my personal comfort levels, I'm pretty sure I don't love others even half as much as I love myself.

My schedule is full and my heart is on lockdown because my world spins on the love I have for myself. All my time and attention is already allocated. I love myself very well—so well that there isn't room or time or effort left to love anyone else. Loving anyone wholeheartedly is an all-in endeavor. This is what Jesus was implying. He is calling us to an all-consuming love. Only he intended the object of our love to be God and others, not self.

Looking into vanity's mirror is a shock to the system. I see my reflection in the Capitol's gross indulgences in *The Hunger Games*. I see it again in the wealthy people in India buzzing about without a second glance at the poorest of the poor lining the streets. I see it every time I retreat to my inner world to tend to my own health and wealth.

These reflections are tough to take in. My gut instinct is to deny and shut down those similarities. I still want to compare myself to the US Joneses so I'll be off the hook, able to continue on with my life. I don't want my comfort habit disrupted.

Denial doesn't change reality, however. The truth is that I am among the haves of the world, with access and ability to do just about any sort of self-improvement my heart desires. My resources aren't limitless, but they are plentiful. I have taken the opportunities my American life affords to produce more opportunities—for myself.

Living for your own glory is the vainest of pursuits. It leaves your life bare and barren. A powerful picture of this sort of living is found in Leviticus. Moses is explaining how God's people are to live in this world, giving practical examples alongside lofty ideals. This one cuts me to the core:

> When you reap the harvest of your land, you shall not reap
> your field right up to its edge, neither shall you gather the

gleanings after your harvest. And you shall not strip your vineyard bare, neither shall you gather the fallen grapes of your vineyard. You shall leave them for the poor and for the sojourner: I am the LORD your God. (Lev 19:9-10)

I am not a farmer; I'm not even a gardener. But this principle of reaping has rich words of wisdom for me in regard to how I gather from the labors of my own life.

When I harvest my life right up to the edges, I have collected every last kernel of blessing. I have stripped every stalk of benefit clean. I have taken all that God has given me and have gathered it up—*for myself*. There is nothing left for anyone else to feast on; there is nothing left to bring comfort to anyone else in need. I harvest my life, collect the yield, bind up the sheaves of bounty, and store it away for my own pleasure.

> **When I harvest my life right up to the edges, I have collected every last kernel of blessing.**

God has given me interests, talents, and gifts to produce a harvest of blessing in this life. Mostly, I have dedicated what I've been given for advancing myself. Intellect and writing talents? I store them up for projects that benefit me. Access to technology and gadgets? I use it to connect with people online to grow my platform. Extra time and health? I invest in my physical appearance. Every inch of my field has been stripped clean; there's nothing left for anyone else.

Having margin is God's idea. I am not supposed to consume every inch of my life for my own benefit. I am not supposed to gather up every piece of fruit. I am not supposed to strip myself bare. I am to have plenty of extra available so that I can freely and readily feed the poor and the sojourner—to extend true comfort to those in need.

False comfort instructs me differently. It tells me to take it all. So I run around the edges of my life and make sure nothing has been left lying about. I hoard my resources in the name of prudence and practicality. I forget that God's ways often defy common sense.

SOMETHING BETTER TO DO

A friend of mine recently made me aware of a thirty-year-old research project on addiction called the Rat Park Experiments. Canadian psychologist Bruce Alexander suspected that previous experiments proving a rat's preference for morphine over water might be affected by its housing conditions. Alexander arranged a luxurious, communal dwelling—dubbed Rat Park—for some rats and provided small, plain, isolated cages for others. Tracking all the combinations of providing water and morphine, Alexander found that isolated rats drank as much as twenty times more morphine than those living in community at Rat Park: "When Alexander's rats were given something better to do than sit in a bare cage they turned their noses up at morphine because they preferred playing with their friends and exploring their surroundings to getting high."[9]

What is true for the rats is true for us. Consumerism is our morphine, cutting the edge of boredom from lives overly fixated on self-improvement and comfort pursuits. Like the rats, we turn to comfort because that's what's available to us; it's what we know. Vanity has sold us a lie about the meaning of life.

The good news is that we too have something better being offered to us. True comfort is here. We no longer need to amuse ourselves with the American dream or self-focused investing. It's time to redeem comfort from these false notions and substitutes. Let's finish clearing the comfort clutter and move on to part two to discover where true comfort is found.

COMFORT CLEANSE

Step 10: Detoxing from the American Dream

Find out how wealthy you are compared to the rest of the world. Visit erinstraza.com/comfort-detox and follow the link to see your place on the Global Rich List.

- Did your results surprise you? If you were to consider yourself wealthy, how might that change the way you extend comfort to those who have less?

- In what ways has the American dream pulled you into a lifestyle that is geared toward improving your own comfort (status, wealth, possessions, etc.)?

- Ask God to show you one thing to adjust in your life to break your comfort habit in this area.

Note: I am in no way endorsing CARE International or asking you to donate to their work.

Step 11: Detoxing from Over-reaping

Make a list of your typical week's events and commitments in the chart. Estimate the time spent on average for each one (your time should add up to 168 hours). A few entries are provided as an example.

Then identify the primary beneficiary for each entry; be as general or specific as you wish. Process with the following questions:

- Do you see any ways that you are overinvesting in yourself?

- How has self-improvement pulled you into a lifestyle that is geared toward improving your own comfort (intellect, experiences, beauty, etc.)?

- In what ways are you over-reaping the harvest of blessing God has poured out on you?

Activity	Hours per Week	Beneficiary
sleeping		
personal care		
exercise		
work		
eating and food prep		
quiet time		
small group		
gardening		
reading		
school		

PART 2

comfort
redeemed

The Comforter

But the Comforter (Counselor, Helper, Intercessor, Advocate,
Strengthener, Standby), the Holy Spirit, Whom the Father
will send in My name [in My place, to represent Me and
act on My behalf], He will teach you all things. And He
will cause you to recall (will remind you of, bring to your
remembrance) everything I have told you.

JOHN 14:26, AMPLIFIED BIBLE
CLASSIC EDITION

If we cooperate with God,
he will take away the natural comforts that
have served us as mother and nurse for so long and
put us where we can receive no help except
from the Comforter Himself.

A. W. TOZER,
THE DIVINE CONQUEST

In the process of dealing with and writing about comfort addiction, I've heard lots of two-minute discourses from people trying to process my two-minute explanation. (Four minutes is just long enough for people to completely misunderstand each other.) Many first responses to the idea of comfort addiction are full of look-over-there examples and look-right-here confessions. I have heard disdain over consumerism, hobbies turned obsessions, daily pick-me-ups, and the lure of Pinterest. These provide surface evidence of the greater issue, which takes more than two minutes to unpack.

For pages now, false comfort has been front and center in this book. Part one was all about putting off the comfort habits that bind us. It was about diagnosis and detoxing, which take time, prayer, and plenty of God's grace.

With some heart clutter now cleared away, we have room to put on new habits, new behaviors, and new truths rooted in God's truth. Part two is all about revelation and renewal. How we need that! For the sort of comfort we're familiar with has skewed how we see the real thing. True comfort is foreign, unfamiliar—so much so that we don't quite know what we are looking for.

The comfort we have become accustomed to gives us two-minute answers and solutions when our needs are cosmic. Our hearts crave true comfort, but finding what our hearts desire will take more than just a few moments of contemplation. It's a lifelong process, one that A. W. Tozer refers to as cooperating with God. And we start by embracing the truth about comfort.

REDEFINING COMFORT

Running errands is one of my least favorite things to do, mostly because shopping is part of the deal. So when I can no longer avoid doing the adult thing, I think through my errands and plan my stops in the quickest route. (This may be the only time I'm efficient.)

One sunny day, I did just that—I had five or six stops organized into a specific route on my index card. I had some favorite music queued and a full water bottle. (I also tried to sport a chipper attitude.

Not sure I accomplished that.) The first stop went smoothly, and I was back in my car on my way to stop two, a shoe store. So far, so good. I wasn't thinking about anything in particular, and I have no idea what music was playing. But as I drove down College Avenue, God spoke.

His voice wasn't so much externally audible as internally present. But I heard him. God cut through my mental chatter and tune singing to say something, to me. The message? *Be ready; Tess will be at the shoe store.*

Here's the backstory: Tess was someone I had not seen in a few years. Our friendship had fizzled out after a series of quite unfortunate, conflict-ridden events that coincided with the darkest years of my life. We didn't have a falling out per se; it was more that our paths needed to separate, and it was made easier when I stepped away from a ministry where we were both involved. It was a difficult, emotionally fraught time with a lot of unrest, especially for me—personality tests cast me as the consummate peacemaker, and in this situation there was no way my friendship with Tess could continue. Seasonal friendships may be a part of life, but to me they feel like unresolved conflict. Which I hate.

All this to say, running into Tess wasn't what I had in mind that day. My first inclination after hearing the news was to brush it away. It was odd. Why would God tell me she would be there? And would she be?

Because it was odd, however, it was actually easier to believe. So I prayed until I got to stop two and went in to look for shoes. Even after roaming all the aisles, I didn't find what I was looking for. I didn't see Tess either. I made my way to the front of the store, turned the last aisle . . . and there she was. *All right then,* I thought. *Here goes. Lord, help me to not be weird.* We greeted each other and shared niceties. I was fairly normal. (I think.) After a few moments we parted ways, and that was it.

Why did God tell me Tess would be at the shoe store? I honestly don't know. Maybe it was just to teach me something crucial about God's heart toward me: he is attentively tender toward all the places in my heart that churn with anxiety and yearn for comfort. By telling me of this encounter, God proved that he goes ahead of me, preparing my steps, waiting for me, extending grace for me to walk through uncomfortable situations. God knows my frame; he knows I am but dust. He knows I need help, and sometimes he will even give me a heads up to show he's got my back. Situations like this prove God's active involvement and infused presence in my everyday life. I wish he would communicate like that more often. Instead, I must exercise my faith that God is going with me, even if he hasn't alerted me to the details of the day's agenda.

When Jesus was nearing the end of his earthly ministry, he gave the disciples a heads up—a bit more grand than the one I received. Soon Jesus would be arrested, put on trial, convicted, and crucified. Soon the disciples would be without the rabbi and friend they had followed for three years straight. I'd classify these events as anxiety producing. Perhaps that's why Jesus alerted his disciples to the agenda that day. He wanted them to know none of it would take him by surprise. He knew what was coming, he knew his earthly ministry was drawing to a close, and he had a plan to share with them:

> But the Comforter (Counselor, Helper, Intercessor, Advocate, Strengthener, Standby), the Holy Spirit, Whom the Father will send in My name [in My place, to represent Me and act on My behalf], He will teach you all things. And He will cause you to recall (will remind you of, bring to your remembrance) everything I have told you. (Jn 14:26 AMPC)

Jesus was returning to heaven, but another was coming to take his place. The Father was sending someone the disciples didn't know, someone who lives up to these amazing descriptive names listed in the

Amplified Bible. This was the Holy Spirit, the one spoken of from ages past. The disciples knew of God's Spirit as the one hovering over the formless earth during creation, the one who is breath and gives life to all, the one who dwelled within certain individuals for God's purposes. They knew of him in theory, but what Jesus was saying was new.

The Holy Spirit would come to pick up the ministry Jesus had started. What Jesus did in his physical body to draw many to the Father, now the Spirit would continue to work out through the hearts of the redeemed. It is an amazing promise, one I'm sure the disciples appreciated but didn't quite understand. Disciples today are still a little foggy on it. Our confusion may be why we keep returning to flimsy comfort substitutes when the real Comforter has promised to be with us.

It floors me that God's Spirit is known as Comforter. Even though we may not quite understand how he works in and through us, one thing we know by now is our deep need for comfort. Our needs for control, space, success, emotional distance, safety, power—these are what we seek to satisfy through various vices. In all these needs, the Comforter offers to be exactly what we require and to soothe whatever rages within our hearts.

The mystery of the Comforter can be scary. The discomfort of the unknown can push us back to what we know—what's comfortable. Known substitutes are easy to grab at a moment's notice, when our stash has been threatened or our boundaries have been infringed upon. Tangible comforts can be stored up, put on a shelf, and pulled out when the desire strikes. Even intangible ones, such as benefits and accomplishments, can be mentally measured and cataloged for future reference. Things, whether tangible or intangible, can be manipulated, controlled, and used—guilt free, no explanation needed, no strings attached.

People, however, cannot be treated like things. And right there is where my comfort pursuits get tied up into a knotted mess. I have pursued the comfort of things, when all along Comfort is a Person. True comfort is our Comforter, the Holy Spirit, wholly God, the third Person of the Godhead.

> **I have pursued the comfort of things, when all along Comfort is a Person.**

Conversely, the things I've leaned on, in A. W. Tozer's words, "as mother and nurse"—all the things detailed in part one—could never possibly satisfy. Inanimate objects have no power; they are completely impotent. False comforts are no more than dumb idols fashioned by human hands.

The good news is that true Comfort, capital C, is alive and well. He is completely able to help me, know me, soothe me, and meet my deepest heart need. And he longs for a relationship with me—and with you. He has come to be exactly what our hearts require, *because that is how God designed us.* Our hearts were meant to function in dependence on God for comfort, counsel, help, intercession, advocacy, strength, and support. Our need for comfort is not the problem; the problem is that we have not gone to the Comforter for what he willingly gives.

What difference would it make if you practiced the habit of depending on the Comforter? Would convenience, safety, and perfection still be so enticing? Would emotional security and acedia be necessary? Would the American dream still be as dreamy? Learning to rely on true Comfort, the Comforter, would upend our old habits and insert a new reward.

Just like any other relationship, it will take some effort to cultivate closeness with the Holy Spirit. If we are to know him, we will have to set our hearts about the task and give him space to function as he is. As Tozer famously said, "The man [or woman] who would know God must give time to him."[1] All relationships—including one with God—are organic. They are either growing or shrinking, getting stronger or weaker. If I have not put in the time, care, or attention to cultivate intimacy with God, my connection to him will be underdeveloped and weak. And how likely is it that I would turn to a practical stranger for help when my comfort alarm sounds? If my relationship with the Comforter is strained, the relational gap makes a substitute more appealing. It's easier to stuff food into my mouth or adorn my body with new clothes or look for affirmation on social media than it is to go to the God of the universe to express my need and ask for help.

Not only is it easier, it's the habit I've nurtured. Choosing lesser things has become second nature. My autopilot has kicked in, leading me to the same old cisterns I've always sought, dry as they may be: "My people have committed two evils: they have forsaken me, the fountain of living waters, and hewed out cisterns for themselves, broken cisterns that can hold no water" (Jer 2:13).

Of course, the Comforter is no less present than these substitutes. But the paths we've worn to the broken cisterns are so very obvious and alluring! We have difficulty seeing and sensing God—much like Jacob, whose life is chronicled in the Old Testament. He lived in acknowledgment of God, the God of his father, Isaac. But Jacob kept God on the fringes, at arm's length—until God spoke to him in a dream one night, affirming he had Jacob's back: "I am the Lord, the God of Abraham your father and the God of Isaac. The land on which you lie I will give to you. . . . Behold, I am with you and will keep you wherever you go, and will bring you back to this land. For I will not leave you until I have done what I have promised you" (Gen 28:13-15).

I wonder whether Jacob's first inclination was to dismiss this news, brush it away. Did he think this was an odd, out-of-the-blue message? Did he wonder why God would tell him this, on this particular night? Perhaps. What we do know is that the dream prompted Jacob to respond in faith; he exclaimed, "Surely the Lord is in this place, and I did not know it" (Gen 28:16).

That's it exactly. Today, right now, God is in this place—with you and me—and we do not know it. This is why we turn to ordinary things for the comfort we need. Tozer says in *The Pursuit of God*, "That was [Jacob's] trouble, and it is ours. Men [and women] do not know that God is here. . . . God is here when we are wholly unaware of it. He is manifest only when and as we are aware of His presence. On our part, there must be surrender to the Spirit of God, for His work is to show us the Father and the Son."[2]

Do we know that God is here? We say we know of Jesus as Immanuel, God with us. But do we believe it? Do I believe God has come to be and stay with me, to the end, no matter what? Do I believe that God is right here, ready to be my comfort in every situation?

Believing this beautiful truth is part of that cooperation process we're in. We must practice seeking God, spending time with him, communing with him. How do we do this? Richard Foster explains in *The Celebration of Discipline*: "We are catapulted into a deep dependence upon the Holy Spirit. After all, if we had a book of rules to cover every circumstance in life, we would not need dependence. . . . He will be to us a present Teacher and Prophet, instructing us in what to do in every situation."[3] Dependence isn't easy. This is why we run from the process of cooperation—we do not want to be in the place where we have to trust God to help us. But this is exactly what we need.

> **Do I believe that God is right here, ready to be my comfort in every situation?**

The day of my Tess encounter I could have refused to cooperate with God, refused to depend on him. I could have skipped that errand. I even could have slipped out of the store without Tess seeing me. These old comfort habits were familiar, easy, engrained. For some reason God gave me the strength that day to say no to control, emotional distance, and the path of least resistance. I learned that God was trustworthy and able to comfort me right when I needed him.

THINKING RIGHT THOUGHTS

It's been so long now, I cannot even begin to count the number of prayers I've prayed. Prayers for direction, peace, wisdom, provision, miracles, patience, joy, trust. I've cried. I've begged. I've proffered deals. After three years of asking for God's intervention, my husband was still struggling with his work. Mike was discouraged, as was I.

But it wasn't always difficult. There was a golden era of sorts, when Mike was running two successful multimillion-dollar businesses—one he launched with a business partner, and one he launched and managed on behalf of a physician group. When business circumstances shifted, Mike sensed change was needed; he sought counsel from trusted men and transitioned out of these businesses he loved, trusting God to lead him into new ventures.

The new ventures were slow in coming. Discouragement and doubt, however, came quickly. Throughout the years I waffled between turning to God for comfort and seeking a quick fix from faulty substitutes. In good stretches, I cooperated with God. I trusted in him to provide and to lead Mike to work he would love. I kept my thoughts captive to the obedience of Christ. I fought discouragement. In weary stretches, however, I shunned the comfort of God. Cookies, shopping, self-pity, control behaviors, emotional distance—all these gave a momentary rush but left me wrung out and empty. The pattern continues for any number of life difficulties I've encountered thus far.

If the end result is less than satisfying, why do I keep falling for it? I can relate to Portia Nelson's poem "Autobiography in Five Short Chapters." In it Nelson describes the experience of walking down a street that has a deep hole. The first time down the road, she's unaware of the hole and falls right in. The second time, she pretends the hole isn't there, falling in again. The third time, she looks at the hole but falls in all the same. The fourth time, she sees the hole and walks far around it so she doesn't fall in. But the fifth time? The fifth time she chooses a different street.[4]

Nelson's poem illustrates what is known as *spiral learning*, a method of teaching that presents concepts in progression rather than all at once. On the first pass the basics are presented. On each successive pass additional material is added to the knowledge base. Learning progresses as a spiral, with deeper learning happening at each round.

Similarly, knowing the Comforter is a progression. Relationships grow with time and interaction. As we walk this life with dark holes of despair, trouble, and trials, we get to know God better as Comforter, learning how to lean on him and find the comfort our hearts need.

Some lessons take much longer than five rounds. We walked enough rounds with Mike's work to lose count and hope. Gratefully, God recently led us down a new road with new work; yet we're still weary, still recovering. Maybe you are weary from the road of infertility or singleness or depression or financial stress. These are rough roads, to be sure.

Over these past three years of unknown, I've wavered and waffled between the Comforter and comfort substitutes—between life and death, blessings and curses. Sometimes I am just plain defiant. Sometimes my emotions hold greater sway than they should. Both of these are sin, placing something else at higher value than God. And both of these are put in their proper place when I see the truth about who God is and trust his heart toward me.

When my time, security, lifestyle, or whatever else is threatened, and all the comfort alarms are squawking inside me, it's tough to think rightly about God. I begin to have suspicious thoughts about his heart. When I jump to conclusions about God, I rarely land on something positive. I jump into thoughts about how God has abandoned me, how he's mad at me, how he's not moved by my plight and pain. And if that's how God is, why would I turn to him for help?

Of course none of these is true, but they *feel* true. Cooperating with God in this process of dependence won't work with thoughts like these. Revelation is needed. Looking again at how Jesus described the Comforter in John 14:26, we see that the Father sent the Comforter to us in Jesus' name. Let that sink in: the Father was so concerned for his beloved—for us—that he sent his Spirit to be with us always. This truth is our first line of defense when our thoughts about God rage negative. But it's not the only truth we have.

God has revealed much about his tender heart toward us. He is merciful and gracious, slow to anger and abounding in steadfast love and faithfulness (Ps 86:15). He will not forget us (Is 49:15). God takes delight in us and rejoices over us with singing (Zeph 3:17). He feels compassion toward us (Mt 9:36). Nothing can separate us from his love (Rom 8:39). Christ became poor so we might become rich (2 Cor 8:9). And here's one of my favorites, a message God instructed the prophet Isaiah to record for him:

> Comfort, comfort my people, says your God.
> Speak tenderly to Jerusalem,
>   and cry to her
> that her warfare is ended,
>   that her iniquity is pardoned,
> that she has received from the LORD's hand
>   double for all her sins. (Is 40:1-2)

God speaks comfort to us, his people. He speaks tenderly to his beloved. He pardons, he blesses. Why don't I jump to conclusions like this about God? If I could grasp even this one message from him, what a difference that would make in my life! Any doubt I have about God's intention toward me would be erased, and I would know God speaks comfort to me, in my darkest hour and for my greatest need.

The Bible is full of God's promises of care and tenderness. And when we get to the Gospels? We are overwhelmed by God's goodness toward us in his Son, Jesus, our Messiah. The Gospels burst with Jesus' acts of compassion, care, and consolation. He was completely in tune with the comfort deficit within every human heart, as he passionately proclaimed: "Come to me, all who labor and are heavy laden, and I will give you rest. Take my yoke upon you, and learn from me, for I am gentle and lowly in heart, and you will find rest for your souls. For my yoke is easy, and my burden is light" (Mt 11:28-30). Coming to Jesus is what we need. We have been yoked to false comfort for so long, and it has forced us to labor unto weariness in its service. Jesus promises that when we come to him, weary as we are with our old ways, he will give us rest. How will he do that?

I referred to Eugene Peterson's answer in the introduction. In his book *A Long Obedience in the Same Direction*, Peterson says we are to be disciples ("people who spend our lives apprenticed to our master") and pilgrims ("people who spend our lives going someplace, going to God").[5] Pilgrims go to Jesus—answering his call to come—and become his disciples by yielding to his wisdom and teaching. The old yoke is removed, replaced by the new, so that we learn to be like Jesus, gentle and lowly in heart (Mt 11:29). Being yoked to pseudo comforts has deadened our hearts to such selfless virtues. Coming to Jesus we receive the comfort of God that softens our hearts, making them pliable into the likeness of Christ, allowing us to be gentle and lowly just as he is.

Nothing else except coming to Jesus has sufficed for me in finding God's comfort in my weariness and discouragement. This coming is where all new habits of faith are introduced, practiced, and established. It is how we will grow to know God for who he really is, not who we have presumed him to be. Running to Jesus makes all the difference in what I think about him. This habit of seeking my Rabbi yokes me to Comfort, reminding me of what's true and thereby dismissing what's false.

I can tell when I've not come to Jesus (and I bet others can sense it too). It has been especially evident in regard to how I respond to the work-related struggle Mike has experienced. Practicing dependence on the Comforter has given me strength to engage with Mike gently instead of turning to acedia's numbing fog. Being yoked to Jesus has taught me to be lowly of heart instead of turning to new stuff to stuff the uncertainties we are facing. Without my coming to Jesus, my old habits and vices would lead me to even greater weariness.

A CLASSROOM IN THE DESERT

Two components of the cooperation process have been discussed so far. The first was the importance of redefining comfort not as things to use but as a Person to seek. The second was the need for thinking right thoughts about God, based on who he has revealed himself to be in his Word. We have one more element of the process: the third component is about renewing the mind. Looking again to Jesus' description of the Comforter in John 14:26, we see his purpose in coming is twofold: to teach us all things and to cause us to recall everything Jesus has said (Jn 14:26).

If the comfort habits I've practiced over the years are to be up-ended, I need to be taught things I do not know and be reminded of things I keep forgetting. Much of the trouble in this learning and remembering is that I'm on autopilot; my routines and habits are so ingrained, I go about my life with a business-as-usual mindset. Revelation is necessary to disrupt this mindlessness, and the Comforter has come for that very purpose.

For many years now, I've gone with friends on an annual weeklong retreat. We take our Bibles, lots of books, and journals to seek God away from the usual happenings of life. It is rich, meaningful time, something I look forward to the entire year, because God uses it to teach me things I wouldn't learn in the midst of my usual routines. Plus, it's at the beach, which is completely unlike the Midwest. A change in scenery is also helpful for seeing old things in a new way.

Each year I become more convinced that retreating needs to be more than a once-a-year event. I need to retreat to God as part of my daily life, even in every moment! But there is something special about stopping the usual routines of life and focusing for a time to learn something new and remember things that have been forgotten. Sometimes we choose the getaway, like with the annual retreat I take with my friends. But sometimes God intervenes rather dramatically to pull us away from our usual lives and teach us something special.

Take for example the way God intervened with the Israelites when they were enslaved in Egypt. God heard their cries for comfort, and he dramatically delivered them, promising to give them special land and new lives. But on the way to the Promised Land he led them into the desert wilderness, where they wandered for forty years, learning to live as God's chosen people. Moses summarized their process of cooperation like this:

> And you shall remember the whole way that the LORD your God has led you these forty years in the wilderness, that he might humble you, testing you to know what was in your heart, whether you would keep his commandments or not. And he humbled you and let you hunger and fed you with manna, which you did not know, nor did your fathers know, that he might make you know that man does not live by bread alone, but man lives by every word that comes from the mouth of the LORD. (Deut 8:2-3)

Did you catch that? God purposefully led the Israelites to wander in the desert for a forty-year lesson. This is both a consolation and a quandary. A forty-year lesson? In the desert? Scripture details their wandering years, and it's not all books and journals and in-depth chats like my beach retreat.

Desert lessons serve a grand purpose, though, for the Israelites and for us. In barren lands God has our full attention, with nothing to distract us. Desert wandering allows us to cooperate with God to put off the old habits we've picked up and put on the new ones that designate us as his beloved.

Although few of us would choose to be humbled, tested, or hungry, we need what comes from that discomfort. Moses said that God led the Israelites so they would know what was in their hearts, whether they would keep his commands or not. The same is true for us: wilderness lessons expose our hearts to the core. No consolations and props are available to distract us or shade the truth: we are a people prone to meeting our base needs with idols and serving self above all else. Without the wilderness, we would not see ourselves as we really are. We would not see the deep, deep need we have for a Savior.

> **Desert wandering allows us to cooperate with God to put off the old habits we've picked up and put on the new ones that designate us as his beloved.**

Deserts aren't devoid of treasure, however. God means to feed our growling bellies with food we know nothing of. He means to give us strength that defies reason. He means to show us his compassion in spite of our self-serving ways.

The wilderness has a special lesson for us about who we are and who God is. In the wilderness we learn anew that God is a loving Father who corrects his children for their ultimate good. In the wilderness we find the comfort our souls have always longed for.

We can count on this: none of the Israelites' wandering was in vain. Not one step was wasted. My friend Wendy and her husband learned this firsthand a few years ago after building their dream home. Nine months after they moved in, her husband began struggling at the job that made the home possible. After much prayer (and amazing answers), they sold the house and moved to the East Coast, where a different job was available. But struggles continued. Financial difficulties, work stress, emotional discouragement—it just didn't let up. Wendy found herself in a barren land—a desert season where the old consolations that had served as "mother and nurse" were stripped away. But that stripping made room for the Comforter to teach Wendy lessons she would not have learned without it. She learned that she doesn't live on the bread of struggle-free days or a beautiful home. In the wilderness, Wendy learned to take God at his word and found a filling she would have never known otherwise.

Lessons like these are precious treasures. When we're in the wilds, the truths are fresh and present. We can't imagine ever growing dull to them! Those lessons do fade, however, after the bell rings our dismissal from the desert classroom. This is why we need reminders, so that what we've learned in the desert doesn't get lost in our regular day to day.

In the Old Testament the Israelites purposed to remember what God was teaching them by building memorials. For example, as Samuel rejoiced in God's deliverance from the Philistines, he built a monument (1 Sam 7). Samuel named it Ebenezer, which means "stone of help." The stone would be a visible reminder to all the people of how God came to their aid.

As I exited one of my darkest desert stretches, a mentor gave me a beautiful doll dressed in bridal finery. Her gift was a modern-day Ebenezer, meant to remind me that God sees me in Christ, as his beloved, spotless bride. For a time I placed this doll where I would see her every day to be reminded of God's love and my new identity in Christ. A glance at the doll would catch my breath, and I would remember all the prayers, help, and hope that came from God through my mentor during an excruciating time.

We need reminders like that. The good news is that the Comforter was sent to remind us of everything Jesus has said—all the lessons, all the truths. The Spirit serves as our constant prompt for all that Jesus has taught us. Our tangible monuments will come and go—like that bride doll—but the Comforter won't let us forget the lessons we've learned in the desert. In this way the Holy Spirit is our ever-present Ebenezer, who reminds us of truth. He is our Stone of Help from ages past, who is always present, always with us, pointing us to truths that have grown fuzzy with time.

In *The Way of the Heart* Henri Nouwen writes, "We have, indeed, to fashion our own desert where we can withdraw every day, shake off our compulsions, and dwell in the gentle healing presence of our Lord."[6] Some deserts choose us; some we can choose for ourselves. What Nouwen speaks of is a purposeful, daily cooperation with God to learn what only the desert can teach us. Fashioning our own desert is a way for us to be alone with God, stripped of all distraction and every comfort that has served as mother and nurse to us.

The desert is where we meet the Comforter, where we practice turning to him to find soothing for our aching hearts. In the desert we can shake off the pseudo comforts we have piled on heavy and high, muffling our heart's true cry for God. We need a desert, where all those compulsions slough off and clear the way for God to teach us, nourish us, and grant us freedom from the habits that bind. Learning to depend on the Comforter, trust his heart, and learn from him is the foundation for transformation. It's like reprogramming our decision matrix. The old ways have been stripped and the truth is installed, preparing us to live out and practice new, life-giving ways instead. Comfort is not what we thought it was—

Comfort is a Person, and he longs to meet with us and make us into his people. He wants to meet us in the desert and make us the comforted.

COMFORT CLEANSE

Step 12: Fashion a Desert

Find a time in the next few days to create your own desert. Carve out an hour (or two or three!) of quiet where you can purposely spend time getting to know our Comforter. Take your Bible and a journal (if you use one), but no electronics. (If you need a timer, find a watch or a clock—or set your phone timer and leave it in the next room where you won't be tempted to access it.)

Read John 14 and work through the following exercises:

- Ask God to reveal the Spirit to you as Comforter, Counselor, Helper, Intercessor, Advocate, Strengthener, and Standby.

- Praise the Father for sending the Spirit to comfort you. Confess the ways you have failed to receive this gift.

- Claim your dependence on the Comforter in learning and remembering truth and experiencing the comfort your heart craves.

- 6 -

The Comforted

Blessed be the God and Father of our Lord Jesus Christ, the Father of mercies and God of all comfort, who comforts us in all our affliction, so that we may be able to comfort those who are in any affliction, with the comfort with which we ourselves are comforted by God.

2 CORINTHIANS 1:3-4

More than 10 million views have been logged for a TED Talk by Nigerian novelist Chimamanda Ngozi Adichie. In "The Danger of a Single Story" Adichie "warns that if we hear only a single story about another person or country, we risk a critical misunderstanding."[1] Adichie clarifies that single stories aren't false; they are true in themselves. The downside of hearing only one story is our willingness to conflate it with holistic, universal truth.

Her theory holds true not only for people or countries but also for ideas. We've heard just one story about the idea of comfort, a single, flat rendition. A US variation. We have a critical misunderstanding of what comfort is, what it's for, how it's meant to be used. We have presumed comfort to be any means by which we soothe ourselves: control over people, places, and things; emotional protective measures and detachment maneuvers; self-seeking life pursuits. This single story has defined and constrained us.

But there are greater truths about comfort we need to hear. There are other stories to consider and take in. The first round was presented in chapter five, debunking comfort as our array of self-soothing substitutes and establishing it as a gift from God—as God himself. The Comforter has come near, ready and willing to meet our deepest heart needs.

And now we embark on the second round of greater truths. Comfort is presumed to be something to gain, use, and hoard for our own personal benefit. But it is so much more! We need to hear the other side of the story. For if we can grasp this truth about comfort, it will go a long way toward correcting the critical misunderstanding brought on by the single stories we've accepted to date.

COLLAPSING INWARD

If our culture could be boiled down to one thing, it would have to be fixation on self. How we look (fashion, fitness, beauty), how our lives are unfolding (convenience, power, security), and how we measure up to others (status, celebrity, wealth) are our constant concerns. The pursuit of pseudo comfort falls right in line. We think we will be happier—more comfortable—by working toward these things. We think one day we'll arrive at the perfect self we've always wanted to be, the perfect life we've always longed for.

It's a modern-day Greek tragedy, echoing the life of Narcissus, one of Greek mythology's best-known characters.[2] There are a few variations of his story, but all have the same components and tragic ending. Narcissus was known for his beauty and extraordinary physique. One day as he leaned over a lake or river to get a drink, he saw his own reflection and became captivated. He discovered how lovely he was and couldn't stop staring at himself. He refused to leave the water's edge. He refused to stop gazing at his own image. He kept on staring . . . until he died. Obsession with self led to Narcissus's demise.

I'm sure it's no surprise that the term *narcissism* originates with this myth. The *New Oxford American Dictionary* says it's an "excessive or erotic interest in oneself and one's physical appearance; extreme selfishness." Narcissism has gotten a lot of press in recent years. Many point to social media as proof that we are more self-obsessed today than ever. The Internet gives us a platform on which we can craft our own image and make it as beautiful as we wish.

A recent biography I read included this cultural commentary:

> It is now become a maxim with some, who are even men of merit, that the world esteems a man in proportion as he esteems himself.... I am often astonished at the boldness with which persons make their pretensions. A man must be his own trumpeter—he must write or dictate paragraphs of praise in the newspapers; he must dress, have a retinue and equipage; he must ostentatiously publish to the world his own writings with his name. . . . He must get his picture drawn, his statue made, and must hire all the artists in his turn to set about works to spread his name, make the mob stare and gape, and perpetuate his fame.[3]

Sounds a lot like Instagram, Twitter, and Facebook, doesn't it? We use them to esteem ourselves, trumpet our accomplishments, make our friends and followers stare and gape, and perpetuate our own fame. But those outlets didn't exist when founding father John Adams wrote this commentary in 1778. His analysis is so spot-on with what we see today, it disproves any notion that people were morally better "back then" or in the "good old days" (whenever that was). The problem of self-obsession isn't new. History tells us otherwise.

Today's social media serves as a dashboard for our hearts, displaying outwardly what we humans have always been captivated by inwardly. Times change, but the human heart has wrestled with self-obsession since before the Greeks crafted the tale of Narcissus.

It began in the Garden with the first people—which means not one person (or generation or era) has ever been free from the lure of fixating on self. The good old days never existed. Adam and Eve's rebellious, sinful choice to turn away from God and choose what seemed right to them is all about the elevation of self over God. In his book *Glory Hunger* pastor J. R. Vassar comments that "Augustine of Hippo described their new, fallen condition as *incurvatus in se*, a turning in on oneself. Adam and Eve curved inward and were no longer living toward God and one another in love but were bent on living for themselves."[4]

Narcissus, Adam and Eve, you and me—we all curve inward, bent on giving self whatever it desires. In regard to comfort addiction, the self dictates our daily choices, refuses to be emotionally vulnerable with others, and consumes life to the full. Like Narcissus, we are so preoccupied with ourselves that we cannot break our gaze from what captivates us; we cannot look around and see that there are other people in our midst. Our insides become like a spiritual black hole, caving ever inward and sucking all energy and light into the collapse.

If we are to survive the force of the black hole and live for something greater than personal comfort, the focus on self must be broken. We must snap the habit of serving self, replacing it with a new habit—a life-giving one that teaches us to live toward others and toward God.

I find this especially difficult to do, as my personality is high on the introvert scale. Being an introvert means that I get refueled by being alone, thinking, reading, and being quiet. It means that being with people and being in public zaps my energy. The good part of introversion is that I enjoy time alone and time with God. Silence and solitude come naturally to me. The bad part is that I too easily turn inward, caving in on myself, focusing on self more than on others.

For ten years I worked as a freelance writer and editor for various clients. The work provided a perfect blend of time alone in my home office and client interaction via meetings and Skype calls. But when my husband's work situation changed a few years ago, my introverted work cocoon changed. Mike moved his office back into our home as well. He, however, is an extrovert, and with the work change his opportunity for social interaction went from thirty people to just one, while my social interaction doubled. The sudden change was difficult for both of us, jarring us out of our preferred workplace scenarios.

A few times each morning and afternoon, Mike would come into my office to chat. It sounds nice, doesn't it? Your love and best friend seeks you out and wants to talk. It was nice—except I wasn't accustomed to the disruption, and it was difficult for me to get back into a writing groove after each visit. I began to panic about meeting deadlines and having more than forty-five minutes of solid writing between chats. That's when those black hole forces would kick in. Anxiety would stir in my heart; the light of good thoughts would dim. I couldn't find my work rhythm, and I handled it terribly. I found it nearly impossible to live toward Mike or God in those moments when my routine was thrown off. My comfort addiction drove me inward to protect what I had planned, to serve my calendar, and to seek control over my time.

My bent toward self revealed the ugliest of who I am. Initially when my comfort and routine were being threatened, I didn't even want to fight against the black hole forces; I simply wanted to stop being interrupted. It took a long time for my heart to yield to God's conviction, but I finally saw this scenario as *incurvatus in se*—I was curving inward, not living outward. I needed to learn a new habit of turning toward God when everything in me was being sucked into the black hole. And I'm still learning, in a two-steps-forward, one-step-back sort of way. The consequences of my cold attitude that bruised my husband's feelings more than once remind me of the harm inward living can cause. Like all other habits, becoming aware of our autopilot is crucial. Awareness of those self-serving patterns helped me tear apart the cue-routine-reward loop and ask God to help me seek a different reward than the one I had grown so fond of.

TURNING OUTWARD

Living for self is the crux of comfort addiction. But comfort addiction is not an impossible habit to kick. In *Counter Culture* author David Platt reminds us of God's rescue that makes such a new habit possible. Platt says that when we no longer seek to serve and soothe self, "our eyes will no longer be focused on what is most comfortable to us; instead, our lives will be fixed on what is most glorifying to God."[5] What freedom this is! When we practice finding our comfort in God, not only will we find the comfort our hearts crave, but we will be free to live for something else. What a relief that God has redeemed us for more than self-centered living!

> **What a relief that God has redeemed us for more than self-centered living!**

Rejoicing in and agreeing with this truth is not the same as living in light of it, however. As true as it is that God's never-ending supply of comfort is always available to us, we have not lived that way. Our patterns of thought and behavior are long ingrained. Our old habits are based on false data, driving us to gather up and protect whatever goods we can get our hands on. This is how I was responding to Mike when he started working from home—I thought I had to fend for myself and protect my stash. But that isn't true at all.

In reality, we have been adopted as God's children, no longer orphans, no longer needing to scavenge for leftover scraps of comfort. We have a loving Heavenly Father who meets our deepest heartfelt needs. And in light of his certain, ongoing provision we are no longer bound to focus on self. We are now free to practice living the truth. We need to learn to live as the rescued. We need to establish new habits to live an outward life. The revelation that I needed to live out of truth instead of lies changed everything. It allowed me to say no to the old habit that was sucking me into the black hole of selfish living and helped me turn outward toward life.

It's time to shift our gaze, to see the world around us, and to be the agents of comfort that God intends us to be. The single story we've heard about comfort has left us short of truth: true comfort is not intended for individual, onetime use. Scripture tells us the fuller story, as Paul described to the believers in Corinth:

> Blessed be the God and Father of our Lord Jesus Christ, the Father of mercies and God of all comfort, who comforts us in all our affliction, so that we may be able to comfort those who are in any affliction, with the comfort with which we ourselves are comforted by God. For as we share abundantly in Christ's sufferings, so through Christ we share abundantly in comfort too. If we are afflicted, it is for your comfort and salvation; and if we are comforted, it is for your comfort, which you experience when you patiently endure the same sufferings that we suffer. Our hope for you is unshaken, for we know that as you share in our sufferings, you will also share in our comfort. (2 Cor 1:3-7)

According to this passage, comfort has a much more robust story than simply serving our self-centered whims and fancies. In the first sentence alone we learn where comfort comes from ("the Father of mercies and God of all comfort"), when God gives it to us ("in all our affliction"), and why God gives it to us ("so that we may be able to comfort those who are in any affliction, with the comfort with which we ourselves are comforted by God"). The comfort of God is beautifully complex. No wonder our pseudo comforts fall flat! They cannot hold up to this sort of rigor.

True comfort enables us to turn outward—toward God for the comfort we need and toward others who need what comes only from God.

STEWARDING COMFORT

A few years ago, I was wrestling with my writing, consumed with fear that my skills were lacking and my ability was scant. Jesus' parable of the talents brought a sense of stewardship to me that affected not only my writing but also every aspect of my life. Jesus tells of a man going on a journey who distributed wages to three servants (Mt 25:14-30). The first servant received five talents (one talent is worth about twenty years' wages), the second received two talents, and the third received one. The first two servants invested their money and increased it. The third, however, "went and dug in the ground and hid his master's money" (v. 18). When the master returned, the first two servants offered the fruit of their investments, and he rewarded them. But the third servant offered only excuses, to which the master replied:

> **True comfort enables us to turn outward—toward God for the comfort we need and toward others who need what comes only from God.**

> You wicked and slothful servant! You knew that I reap where I have not sown and gather where I scattered no seed? Then you ought to have invested my money with the bankers, and at my coming I should have received what was my own with interest. So take the talent from him and give it to him who has the ten talents. For to everyone who has will more be given, and he will have an abundance. But from the one who has not, even what he has will be taken away. (Mt 25:26-29)

The sort of stewardship Jesus speaks of is about more than financial investments. In regard to my writing, I think of it in terms of skill that God has entrusted to me. It may be just one talent's worth, but I want to invest that one talent wisely. I refuse to bury it. I refuse to curve inward. My master has entrusted this one to me to steward, and I intend to invest it and multiply it.

Likewise, God has distributed a measure of comfort to each one of us, and he has an expectation of return. According to Paul's description in 2 Corinthians, comfort is not meant to be hoarded or buried in the ground but to be passed along "so that we may be able to comfort those who are in any affliction, with the comfort with which we ourselves are comforted by God." God distributes his comfort expecting us to pass it on and to serve others with what we've been given. Comfort is never meant for a single, onetime use. It grows in power when we pass it on.

God grants comfort to our aching souls so that we will recycle it for others who are aching. When God sends his comfort into the world through his people, they are to keep it moving for the greatest impact. It's the difference between a stream and a pool of still water. Water that stands still is likely to become stagnant and stale, a cesspool that isn't good for anyone. True comfort is more like an ever-flowing stream. It isn't stagnant. True comfort is sent out to do a full work, ever on the move, never landing in one place for too long.

In my comfort-addicted state, I have failed to invest the comfort God loaned to me. My pursuit of natural comforts had left me bloated, sluggish, and unable to see beyond myself. (And still not satisfied.) Whatever comfort I did receive from God was going to waste because I was not paying it forward and letting it do a greater work.

This mirrors how the Israelites rebelliously hoarded manna during their desert stint (see Ex 16:15-20). God had led his stubborn people to wander the desert, but he lovingly cared for them, meeting their needs in miraculous ways. He promised that every morning the ground would boast a dew-like covering of bread from heaven. The people were to collect the food, but only what was needed for that day and no more. Of course, some Israelites collected more than they needed; they were hoarding God's provision. The practice was futile. The Israelites found that yesterday's stash of bread was always rotten. Hoarding God's provision simply doesn't work.

The same can be said of God's provision of comfort. If we gather God's gift in excess, hoarding it for future use, it will turn stale. Whatever I refuse to share today, right now, in the moment, will decay and spoil. And if I attempt to keep myself satisfied from my poisoned stash, my heart will eventually take ill, suffering from greater and deeper bouts of selfishness.

God is gracious enough to give us comfort in our time of need. It is meant to do a double work, though: first to comfort us in our afflictions, and second to comfort others in theirs. It is to be in motion, kinetic. Our culture's individualistic mindset doesn't help us in comfort's pay-it-forward process. We are not attuned to thinking about the collective. So when Paul speaks of comfort being a two-step process that is partly about God comforting us and partly about us comforting others, it's not an easy leap. I greatly appreciate Matthew Henry's commentary on 2 Corinthians 1:3-7:

> First, this provision of comfort is not self-serving but is intended to equip for service to the church. God comforts us, Paul states, so that we, in turn, can *comfort those in any trouble* (v. 4). The trouble may vary (the sense is "whatever the trouble") but the comfort remains the same. *So that we can comfort* points to the fact that the means God uses to provide encouragement is other people. This was certainly the case in Paul's life. It is easy to talk about divine comfort in the abstract, but for Paul, God's comfort was very real. It was

something he received with Titus's arrival from Corinth (7:6) and something he experienced on hearing the good news about the Corinthian church (7:4). In turn, the comfort that he gained when "harassed at every turn" (7:5) prepared him to give encouragement to those around him (1:5). Suffering, then, is a training ground for service to the body of Christ. It equips us so that we can better minister to those who, for the sake of the gospel, are going through trials and hardships. In this way we mediate God's encouragement.[6]

Henry's perspective elevates the purpose of comfort to epic proportions. In the life of a believer, God comforts us so we are trained and ready to serve the body of Christ for the sake of the gospel. Without this perspective, the comfort God extends only lands in the cesspool and soon spoils. Comfort hoarded is comfort squandered, wasted.

God has so much more in mind! He invites us to be agents of his comfort, meeting whatever needs people have when they encounter any sort of trouble. We are his ambassadors, sent as his representatives, *for the sake of the gospel*.

The way that we respond to a world in need puts the gospel on display. When we extend comfort from our places of need, we proclaim that God's healing is sure, even when we aren't fully healed yet. When we give away comfort instead of hoarding it, operating from a place of abundance rather than scarcity, we lift high the power of the gospel.

What would it be like if we purposed to walk out the twofold comfort process? Comfort would abound.

BECOMING WOUNDED HEALERS

Years ago I attended a women's retreat. Over the course of the weekend, God's presence became more pronounced. By the last session, there was an outpouring of heartfelt sharing and raw honesty. Pains, sins, and struggles were confessed. Prayer, tears, and love were given. It was a true gift.

As my friends and I made our way home, we discussed the miracle of such walls-down conversation. One friend lamented the amount of time it took for women to get real, wishing we had started the weekend with that level of honesty. Janet proposed a facetious solution: our nametags should have simply listed our wounded places, and then we could have gathered into groups to help each other heal. Cheeky as the suggestion was, I have never forgotten it.

Forced transparency would likely scare attendees away. But our need for raw honesty and comfort from others remains. Each one of us has encountered pains in this life, many of which trip our obsessive need for comfort. We all have those "scorched places" that Isaiah speaks of (Is 58:11). If this is our common experience, why do we tend to hide it?

Something has taken over in our Christian circles that prevents us from regularly experiencing such depths of transparency that my friends and I shared at the retreat. It is the assumption that scorched places detract from our Christian witness, that we must show the world Jesus is true by our now-perfect lives. Michael Horton, in his book *Christless Christianity*, argues otherwise: "Hypocrisy is especially generated when the church points to itself and to our own 'changed lives' in the promotional materials."[7] I flee transparency when I erroneously assume that my job is to prove Jesus is true by the pristine nature of my life.

The truth is, I have scorched places in my life that have produced much pain and shame. This is why I am desperate for the Comforter, and why I am ecstatic the gospel is true. My need for the gospel doesn't fade the longer I walk with Jesus; rather, I become more and more aware of the depth of my need and the astounding love of God that comes to heal my scorched heart. God gives dignity to our broken places, our weak spots, our raw and red patches. He beckons us to come out of hiding so he can generously apply a healing balm.

We hide out of a desire for emotional security, and acedia helps us with that effort by numbing us and encouraging us not to care about the plight of others. If we are going to live outward lives, however, we cannot keep hiding. John's first letter to the early church explains why hiding isn't an option for us: "God is light, and in him is no darkness at all. If we say we have fellowship with him while we walk in darkness, we lie and do not practice the truth. But if we walk in the light, as he is in the light, we have fellowship with one another, and the blood of Jesus his Son cleanses us from all sin" (1 Jn 1:5-7). Fellowship with God and others is only possible when we are walking in the light, being honest about our broken, needy places.

Jesus also taught that honesty is needed to receive the comfort of God: "Blessed are those who mourn, for they shall be comforted" (Mt 5:4). And so we must be real enough to mourn our pains, losses, betrayals, and disappointments—our scorched places. It's when I choose to hide or deny my pain that comfort substitutes look appealing. Those substitutes, as we saw in part one, are futile helpers. Only those brave enough to mourn will be truly comforted.

When I go to God with my wounds and afflictions and receive his comfort, I have something worthwhile to pass on. My wounded places become founts of comfort to others—something I would never have believed possible. Henri Nouwen's *The Wounded Healer* explains: "Making one's own wounds a source of healing, therefore, does not call for a sharing of superficial personal pains but for a constant willingness to see one's own pain and suffering as rising from the depth of the human condition which all men share."[8]

We do not need to match up wound to wound with others for comfort to be shared. Wounds are unique; therefore, the comfort I may need in a betrayal is unlike the comfort you may need in your betrayal. But that doesn't mean we cannot be of help to one another. Our losses make us like Jesus, wounded healers who long to show compassion to others.

One of my scorched places is infertility. Mike and I had to walk the road of testing and treatments in an attempt to have a child. We were placed in the mystery category, meaning there was no diagnosable reason why we were not getting pregnant. After a few years of appointments and needles and procedures with no progress, I was done. I was tired of getting my hopes up when sonograms showed bulging ovaries and blood tests showed skyrocketing hormones. I was tired of hopes deflating each month when none of our efforts resulted in a pregnancy. So we took a break from the pursuit and grieved what wasn't. In time we arrived at a peaceful place, content with the life God had given us, even though it didn't look like the life we had imagined for ourselves.

Grief isn't fun. It hurts to name what was lost and to mourn what will never be. We had to face all that in our infertility, not once, but any time childlessness pounced on us to punch us in the gut—again. Pregnancy announcements, baby showers, adorable kids, family gatherings, baby dedications at church on Mother's Day and Father's Day—all these brought new bouts of sadness. Mourning is a lot of work.

Into this scorched place, God has given comfort beyond measure. I have no explanation for the peace I have about a life that isn't the norm. Fresh waves of disappointment come, to be sure, but I go back to the memorials established here, and the Comforter reminds me that he is bigger than my childless ache.

The beautiful thing about God's comfort is that it has endless applications. The comfort I've received for infertility isn't only for the childless, it's for all who face a life different from the one they expected: the singles who wish to be married, the married who are lonely in marriage, the betrayed who have been abandoned, the aimless who don't sense God's leading, the poor who struggle every single month to pay bills, the anxious who can't imagine why life has to be this difficult. As God leads others to my scorched land, I have the honor of sharing the comfort that abounds here. The same is true for your scorched places—God's power truly is made perfect in our weaknesses (2 Cor 12:9).

Sadly, I haven't always shared God's comfort or welcomed others into my wounded territory. Sometimes I forget that to give is better than to receive. Sometimes my heart is numbed out, callous, refusing to engage with the needs of others. Sometimes I don't want to stop to help the poor soul who has been sidelined, beaten down by life. But Paul's description of comfort for the Corinthians doesn't even consider a one-stop possibility. Comfort is always something given to us so that we can give it away.

If we are to follow in Jesus' footsteps as wounded healers, comfort must be kept in motion. And when we refuse to pass it along? Comfort that stalls out in our hearts is a double loss: it robs others of a healing balm and it robs us of a full measure of comfort. What if in all our hoarding we have only received half of comfort's benefits? According to Paul, comfort is always a twofold process, first of receiving and second of giving. It's possible that the act of giving away comfort from the very afflictions we've endured brings an even greater solace. Comfort is actually multiplied in the giving and reduced in the keeping.

Comfort is actually multiplied in the giving and reduced in the keeping.

PASSING IT ON AND PAYING IT FORWARD

The beauty of the gospel is that Jesus is Immanuel, God who came to be with us in our suffering. As the Man of Sorrows, he is our Wounded Healer. He sympathizes with our weaknesses. He grieves our brokenness. He extends to us the comfort we were designed for, restoring us fully to the Father through his wounds. In Christ our scorched places receive comfort and will one day be fully redeemed.

Until then, God invites us to be his agents of comfort. We get to be his hands and feet on earth, proving that hope in the Messiah is not in vain. David Platt is right: our reward for proclaiming and living in light of this hope is greater than anything our culture could ever offer us. Our culture—and our sin nature—has formed and shaped us to live toward self. Instead of curving inward, however, the Wounded Healer frees us to lean toward others with all of ourselves. We bring our wounds, our brokenness, and our sorrows to the world, and through them we offer others the comfort God has given us. Comfort will come through these scorched places where God's care has settled into our hearts, softening us with his tender care. Here we find rest in God's love, with no need for pretense, no need to tell a story of perfection. What freedom we gain when we can be our true selves! And what blessing others gain when we no longer hide behind impenetrable facades. Only the full story of God's comfort provides the truth that sets everyone free.

The truth of the gospel is what transforms comfort hoarders like you and me into comfort agents worthy of the King. Transformation comes in embracing the full story of God's comfort: comfort is experienced in full when it is received with joy and shared freely with others. As we close part two of this book, these are the new habits that will free us to keep watch with others and experience the full measure of God's comfort.

COMFORT CLEANSE

Step 13: The Full Story

Visit erinstraza.com/comfort-detox and follow the link to watch the TED Talk by Nigerian novelist Chimamanda Ngozi Adichie titled "The Danger of a Single Story."

- What did you learn about the danger a single story can have for our opinions and views?

- How has the single story you've heard about comfort shaped your desire for and pursuit of comfort?

Step 14: Comfort Inventory

Sit with God and ask the Comforter to remind you of all the ways his comfort has gone into your scorched places. Write down what you are reminded of and ask God to show you how you can pass this comfort on to someone else in need.

PART 3

comfort
set loose

Free

*You and I were created for more than filling
up our schedules with the self-satisfying
pursuits of personal pleasure.*

PAUL DAVID TRIPP,
A QUEST FOR MORE

The Question wasn't being mean by pouncing on me. I know that now. What I interpreted as a hissing attack was really passionate urgency. The *what-am-I-doing* inquiry sought to gain my attention for my own good. It meant to awaken me from my comfort-induced stupor so I could live fully, on purpose, engaged.

In *A Quest for More* Paul David Tripp affirms that we were made for more than cramming our days full with routines, habits, and patterns to keep our comfort zones in place: "We were not wired to be fully satisfied with self-survival and self-pleasure. God purposed that the borders of our vision would be much, much larger than the boundaries of our lives."[1] Small living isn't the point of a human life. If you think about it, being comfortable isn't exactly exciting. Being comfortable is akin to being relaxed, at rest, static, motionless, inert—*lifeless*. That's not the sort of life I want to live.

Yet a body at rest will stay at rest until a greater force comes along and pushes it into motion. The Shredding and The Question worked in tandem to kick my life into gear. Together they cleared away old habits to establish truth in my decision matrix so that new habits could be formed—ones that would be life giving, to me and to those around me.

If comfort is a mindless habit, we need what Paul described in Romans 12:2: "And do not be conformed to this world, but *be transformed by the renewing of your mind*, so that you may prove what the will of God is, that which is good and acceptable and perfect" (NASB, emphasis mine). The gospel is the reset button our minds need. Three of those old, world-conforming habits were identified in chapter two: convenience, safety, and perfection. The gospel overpowers each one by introducing new habits to override the old. Compassion, trust, and humility are the life-giving habits we need in order to walk free from the destructive habits that bind us.

COMPASSION OVER CONVENIENCE

It was only noon, but I was already zapped of energy. Work was piled high. I could see there were more things to do than hours remaining in the workday. But I couldn't work late because I also needed to put in a few hours of writing that evening. Once again Mike would be sacrificing for me, because these two commitments alone (work and writing) required the bulk of my waking hours. The collective weight of these burdens may not seem like much, but something about these pressures always works against my introverted personality. I appreciate Susan Cain's push for a Quiet Revolution (QuietRev.com), a recognition that introverts are wired to prefer environments that are calm and less stimulating.[2] Days that are frenzied and overly stimulating are my version of the children's story about Alexander's terrible, horrible, no good, very bad day.[3]

For me, days like this are a perfect storm for slipping into old comfort habits. Stress prompts me to live for whatever will make things more convenient, more streamlined, more comfortable. But it's right there, in the stress, that God wants to pour out his comfort so I can live free from the lure of doing only what's easy and convenient. I needed him on this particular day when I had too much to do. Because that day I got a phone call from a friend in need, and I had a choice to make: to live for convenience or to live for compassion.

Jesus faced lots of less-than-convenient moments in which people clamored for his time and attention. They disrupted him without regard for his energy level or schedule. In Luke 5:17-26, Jesus was teaching a very large crowd and the religious elite were present. In the middle of his message, a ruckus turned all eyes upward as the roof was peeled back by a group of men who then lowered their paralytic friend through the hole to place him right in front of Jesus. This was inconvenient timing, disrupting Jesus' sermon and all.

In that moment Jesus had to seek the Spirit's wisdom for how he was to respond. Was his mission to complete the sermon? If so, that paralytic man would have to wait for the next available slot in Jesus' healing calendar. But if Jesus' mission was to show the compassion of God to the least in the world, this interruption was more like a divine appointment. Jesus rolled with the moment; instead of being frustrated with the inconvenience, he was moved with compassion by the faith of these men for their friend. He spoke to the paralytic's most urgent need—forgiveness—stirring up the ire of the crowd.

In my introverted world, this environment was anything but calm and serene. First the sermon was interrupted, then the religious VIPs were angered by the illustration. Not quite how I would have envisioned the day going had I been the one teaching. Isn't it fascinating that Jesus was subject to the unexpected and unplanned elements of everyday life, just as we are? I'm guessing the disruptions Jesus experienced were no less inconvenient than ours, and he too had to stop and seek the Spirit's guidance. Even the Son of God did not have a play-by-play agenda to work from. Even Jesus was tempted to say no to the inconvenience of need, just as I was when my friend called on that terrible, horrible, no good, very bad day.

I could tell something was wrong the moment I heard her voice. Between sobs, she asked whether I might have time to meet, because something terrible had happened and she needed someone to talk to. Despite the feelings I had formed about my day to that point, it was serene compared to my friend's. I was immediately overcome with compassion for her and her pain. There was no question: work and writing could wait. My friend needed me.

Is this how Jesus saw people? Is this how he sees us? As friends in dire need? Maybe that's how he was able to press on in compassion, even though there were always more people to help, feed, heal, teach, and love. He was free from the need to make his day easier because compassion won out. How I want that freedom! So I've been practicing compassion to combat the lure of convenience. It isn't a once-and-done act but an ongoing death to self—every day choosing to do what Jesus would do.

Learning the new habit of compassion disrupts the bent we all have toward serving our own preferences and taking the path of least resistance. What was it that Jesus said about that? "Then Jesus told his disciples, 'If anyone would come after me, let him deny himself and take up his cross and follow me. For whoever would save his life will lose it, but whoever loses his life for my sake will find it. For what will it profit a man if he gains the whole world and forfeits his soul? Or what shall a man give in return for his soul?'" (Mt 16:24-26).

> **Learning the new habit of compassion disrupts the bent we all have toward serving our own preferences and taking the path of least resistance.**

Deny yourself. Take up your cross. Follow Jesus. None of these are very convenient. Jesus is clear: the gospel is not about conserving your life, but spending it, for his sake. Divine appointments give us the opportunity to gain life by denying our self-focused plans and preferences.

A prominent value in US society is efficiency. We strive to find better ways of getting things done to make things more convenient. Great benefits come from these qualities, and Scripture often lauds them. But God's people are to serve him above efficiency. Our well-laid plans are to yield to God's intervention, which is a challenge. Author Tim Challies touches on this in his book *Do More Better*: "Pride may make you so convinced that you already know the best direction for your day that you will say no to everything, not letting even God himself interrupt your plans with something so much better than what you had plotted out."[4]

Divine appointments will come whenever God so chooses—not necessarily when you are feeling equipped, rested, or ready. They will come in the middle of your terrible, horrible, no good, very bad day. They will challenge your schedule, frustrate your plans, and disrupt your calm. What we lose in these inconveniences, however, is nothing compared to what we gain.

Divine appointments remind us that God has an eternal agenda. He isn't looking for the equipped, rested, or ready to do his bidding. He's calling people like us, the feeble and weary, because he intends to give us everything needed to fulfill his plan. His comfort supply is unending. Yielding to God's disruptions will make your ordinary day—even your terrible, horrible, no good, very bad day—into something memorable. God's inconveniences will align your schedule and plans to his. Divine appointments give you the blessed opportunity to serve Jesus by serving the least around you.

Jesus is our example, showing how to set aside agendas, plans, and even personal desires to impress the masses so that we might be his agents of comfort. Our acts of sacrifice extend compassion to those in need and display evidence to a watching world that

God is true. A disciple's life is one that is spent in full. We are to break open our lives—the life jars discussed in chapter two—like Mary broke open her alabaster jar, pouring out every drop of ourselves in a fragrant act of worship.

Choosing whatever is easiest for me is my autopilot mode. It's a habit. Divine appointments have come, and I have often dismissed them without thinking. That's why awareness is so important. Being aware that my first impulse just may be the wrong choice is a helpful first step. Learning a new habit starts here, in the pause, where I at least entertain the possibility that I should do the opposite of my first reaction. Then the Spirit has a chance to interrupt my long-established comfort habits and begin replacing them with a new habit driven by compassion for others.

Considering the opposite is what my dear friend Janet did when a request was made of her time. A woman asked her for a ride to and from their weekly AA meeting. To comply Janet would have to alter her pattern, go out of her way, and add extra time into her already-full schedule. The status quo was screaming at Janet to say no. After some contemplation, Janet decided to forgo the easy route and committed to helping this woman. What was the tipping point? Janet says that compassion won out over convenience. This woman's license had been revoked; without a ride to AA, she might skip the group, placing her in danger of relapse. Janet was overcome with compassion for her predicament, and that motivated Janet to do what was inconvenient.

These are the everyday sorts of decisions that inspire me to pour out my life for others. By becoming suspect of my first responses—often ruled by whatever is most convenient—I give the Spirit a chance to influence me. I give the Spirit time to reroute me, to disengage the autopilot that kicks in with the strongest habits I've formed. It gives me the chance to live a life of worship.

TRUST OVER SAFETY

Worship is key in the life of a Christian. And it begins with faith: "Without faith it is impossible to please [God], for whoever would draw near to God must believe that he exists and that he rewards those who seek him" (Heb 11:6). Unless we trust God, we will never worship him rightly.

Trust is a tricky thing. Most of us would consider ourselves trusting. I know I do. But then some situation arises that requires me to act on my trust, and I realize how feeble it really is. Last summer my husband and I had the pleasure of hosting a yard dog, and it became a real-life illustration of how trust works. Maybe you haven't heard of a yard dog before; this is what we called the dog that adopted our yard for daytime lounging. She was small, sort of Pomeranian/Chihuahua-looking thing. Every few days we would find her snoozing on our shady deck or curled up on our front porch. We tried to coax her over to check her collar, but she would have none of that. Whenever we went outside and called to her, she would trot away. We didn't know her owners, but she looked cared for; we assumed she just liked our quiet yard. Her visits were amusing, and she wasn't bothering us. I liked having her around, even though she refused to be friends.

But soon she was showing up every day, and we worried she might be lost. Then a pet-loving neighbor left us a note because she was very concerned that we were leaving "our dog" out in a storm and in the heat. She wondered whether we realized "our dog" was getting outside every day. We felt terrible! So we contacted our local animal rescue group, and they brought out a cage and filled it with bacon, assuring us it would not attract every wild animal in the neighborhood. Our yard dog followed bacon's siren call as expected, and once the cage's trapdoor shut behind her, she whimpered and shook with fear, scratching at the edges trying to get out. We went to calm her, but she growled and snarled at us. The rescue group said this reaction was common because dogs on the run lose their trust of humans in just a few weeks' time. This poor thing had probably been roaming for almost six weeks. All trust was gone.

When our yard dog was on the loose, she didn't need to trust us. She benefited from our yard and shade. We watched over her from afar because she refused to come near. Her lack of trust made the situation impossible: we couldn't take care of a yard dog that wouldn't let us care for her. And once she was trapped, the bacon feast and water did little to calm her nerves. She didn't know us and didn't trust that we had good in mind for her.

The analogy isn't perfect, but our comfort habits turn us into fearful yard dogs. We do not trust God's heart toward us. We refuse to draw near to God, refuse to believe who he is, refuse to trust he has good in mind for us. How desperate we are for the transformation Paul spoke of in Romans 12:2!

Establishing new patterns of trust takes time and effort. Our brains need to be rewired so that our first inclination isn't maintaining our preconceived—and erroneous—notions of personal safety. For example, most of us presume we are most safe the closer we are to home. But it is widely reported that nearly one in three car accidents happen less than one mile from the driver's home, and another third happen between one and five miles from home. In an article for *The Telegraph*, Brian Martin explains that "many drivers appear to be in a comfort zone when driving close to home on familiar roads, hence why such a large proportion of accidents occur there."[5]

Staying safe isn't a matter of staying within our comfort zones. (And when it comes to car accidents, it looks like the comfort zone is actually more dangerous because we are in an autopilot fog.) Being safe doesn't depend on exercising common sense and staying close to what's comfortable. Corrie ten Boom, a Nazi concentration camp survivor, gives this powerful example from something her sister Betsie once said: "There are no 'ifs' in God's world. And no places that are safer than other places. The center of His will is our only safety."[6] Only by following God "where my trust is without borders," as described in the song "Oceans" by Hillsong, will I be in the safest possible place.[7] So really, if I'm going to be driven by my bent toward safety, I must follow God wherever he leads, even into places that don't *look* safe. I will actually need to say no to comfort if I'm going to enjoy true safety.

Katie Davis Majors is a woman whose trust is without borders. When she was eighteen years old she left her family and home in Tennessee and moved to Uganda to teach kindergarten for a one-year term. The overwhelming needs she saw prompted her to remain in this unknown, unfamiliar place, to do whatever she could. She established a child sponsorship program. She created a non-profit organization named Amazima. Then she adopted thirteen girls. None of this was safe or comfortable, but she determined to stay in the middle of God's will, doing whatever she sensed Jesus would do. She explains, "We are not called to be safe, we are simply promised that when we are in danger, God is right there with us. And there is no better place to be than in His hands."[8]

How I want to live like this! When I read of someone like Katie, it's tempting to look at her life and presume that we should all move to Uganda, start a nonprofit, and adopt a dozen-plus children. Perhaps. Perhaps that is what God has in mind. But formulaic living is its own sort of comfortable. Legalistic rules for living free can heap on guilt and confuse courage with adherence to a checklist of external actions. We cannot presume God has the same sort of life in mind for each of us. So what does God have in mind? To find out, we have to do the hard work of seeking the Spirit and then following wherever he leads. He may take us to Uganda. He may lead us across town or across the street.

He may even lead us into seasons of barrenness. I know this one firsthand. Mike and I have been wading through his difficulties with work and calling for the past few years. It is a desert land with few consolations. The ongoing struggle has required me to practice the habit of trust. Old habits would have me run to my comfort zone for the protection and security I could find in quick-fix substitutes. I'm an idea gal, so I have all sorts of solutions: *Let's move! Let's launch a business! Go back to school! Start a nonprofit! Become missionaries!* All these sound fun and would provide a welcome oasis of purpose and escape from the scorching desert of this unknown stretch. But I have no idea whether God would have Mike do any of these things. Instead of pushing my bright ideas, I have to practice running to God for the comfort I need so that I can pass that comfort on to Mike. Mike doesn't need my Pollyanna recommendations. He needs to see me resting in God's promises for us. Practicing trust means that I have to confront my doubt that God's promises are true—regardless of the circumstances, regardless of the lack of security I may feel in the wasteland we find ourselves stuck in.

> **Practicing trust means that I have to confront my doubt that God's promises are true—regardless of the circumstances, regardless of the lack of security I may feel.**

For example, I have to process whether I really believe God's heart toward us matches how he reveals himself in Isaiah 41:9-10:

> "You are my servant,
>   I have chosen you and not cast you off";
> fear not, for I am with you;
>   be not dismayed, for I am your God;
> I will strengthen you, I will help you,
>   I will uphold you with my righteous right hand.

God spoke these words to Isaiah more than two thousand years ago, but God does not change. He is the same yesterday, today, and forever. And if I am to worship God for who he has revealed himself to be, I must believe what these verses tell me about God's character toward his people in general and toward me in particular: *God has chosen me. God hasn't cast me off. He is with me. He is my God. He will strengthen me. He will help me. He will uphold me with his righteous right hand.* If I can practice this sort of trust in God, I am free from needing to stay in my comfort zone to protect myself. I don't have to behave like our yard dog, all skittish and mistrusting. If this is true about God, I don't need to know the exit strategy from the desert and I don't need to arrange a solution for my troubles. If this is true, I am free to follow God's lead even to places that look unsafe or unappealing.

If this is true about God, it frees me to keep watch with Mike in his sorrow. I don't have to run away from trouble, for God is with me and won't abandon me. And because he is my God, I worship him by comforting Mike, who certainly feels like one of the least in this world. I can practice trusting this God who has promised to meet my needs as I draw near to him, believing he exists just as he has said, believing he rewards those who seek him for help.

Practicing trust isn't easy. It's a mental battle, one of taking thoughts captive and refusing to give in to lies. When my trust for God is without borders, I am free to keep watch with those in need of comfort, despite unappealing or unsafe circumstances, because the God of all comfort is with me.

HUMILITY OVER PERFECTION

Dependence on God is beautiful. But it is otherworldly. In this world, flawless independence is revered. Society loves to elevate mere humans to near idol status (only to rejoice when they prove to be less than perfect). I have played the game, buying into the false comfort a flawless life seemingly provides. It lures me to project a super-spiritual persona to the world, a life perfected and smooth, with no rough edges or mistakes as far as the eye can see.

Facades leave us hollow and lonely, though, unable to get beyond our own ruse to be of any help to others. We need the opposite habit of humility to override our perfectionistic ways if we are to become God's comfort agents to a world in need. Humility allows us to lower our shields and risk being less than perfect so we can be something more worthwhile: real. Authenticity is all the rage these days, probably because we've seen enough shams to be suspicious when things look too good to be true.

> **Humility allows us to lower our shields and risk being less than perfect so we can be something more worthwhile: real.**

For more than a year now I've cohosted the podcast *Persuasion* with Hannah Anderson. We discuss current events, perplexing issues, and cultural happenings. It's been a joy. But it's also been the weekly reminder I need for practicing humility. Although the show isn't aired live, we try to keep the discussion real with as few edits as possible. We prepare a list of talking points and then hit record. Each week I am faced with the reality that I do not know everything. I'm learning to think on the fly and be okay with comments lacking nuance or expertise.

The anxiety I feel just before recording churns up my insides, scatters my thoughts, and quickens my breathing. It isn't exactly easy. But I am forced to practice humility, recognizing that I am a work in progress; I have not arrived. Not only have I not arrived, I will not get beyond where I am without practicing humility. As Jocelyn Glei writes, "If you refuse to put yourself in a situation where you might give an imperfect performance, you'll prevent yourself from receiving the proper feedback, input, and direction necessary for additional growth."[9]

Refusing to say no to perfectionism costs more than personal growth, however. It also prevents us from being real enough to meet others in their point of need. The purpose of *Persuasion* is to inspire listeners to think and wrestle through tough topics of our day. If I refused to host the show in order to protect my pride, I would lose out on the opportunity to present ideas and nurture discussion with a wide array of people. Am I willing to put aside my desire to present a flawless self for the greater good of building into others?

Humility is essential for overcoming perfectionism. Andrew Murray, in his classic book titled simply *Humility*, describes humility as a person "simply acknowledging the truth of his position as creature, and yielding to God His place."[10] Only God is to be revered, honored, and praised. And this truth frees me from needing to be seen as having my life all together. The pseudo comfort of perfection can be set aside, and I can be who I am: a sinner, saved by grace. It is humility that allows me to be honest about my imperfections and my need for all the comfort God can supply. Humility enables something real and true to thrive. Humility invites others into that real space to receive real comfort for real needs.

Humility allows us to be who we are (needy, imperfect creatures) so that Jesus can be who he is (Provider and Creator). Everything is in its proper place. Because of Jesus, we no longer need to be perfect. Knowing who we are—imperfect, yet beloved—and knowing who God is—perfect, all-loving—frees us to know and share true comfort.

It is still tempting at times to shy away from my flaws and failures, despite all I'm learning through podcasting—and through my cohost, Hannah. Her latest book is about humility, and I've learned so much from her about why it's such a rarity:

One of the main reasons we struggle to create safe communities is because we've underestimated God's power in brokenness;

we've failed to believe that his "power is made perfect in weakness." And so we trust in ourselves. We can never admit failure. We can never admit need. We can never be weak. But it is precisely our brokenness that humbles us, and it is precisely our brokenness that reveals God's power. In II Corinthians, the Apostle Paul writes about how the power of Christ rested upon him because of—not in spite of—his weakness.[11]

If I am to give God's power center stage, I need to be real about my brokenness, real about my neediness. In the moment, though, when it's time to be real like that, it's a battle. I was with some colleagues for a meeting and we split into small groups to pray for our work and each other. Two younger women and I huddled up to share requests. I was having a rough day—I was exhausted from editing this book and from the desert of Mike's work life. I needed support and prayer, but I was so tempted to be vague because thoughts like these were assaulting me: *What if they think I'm a spiritual wimp? What if they pity me? What if I look stupid?* False comfort was offering the easy route—to maintain the illusion of spiritual piety. But the Comforter pressed me to acknowledge the truth: I really *was* discouraged and weary; I really *was* needy; I really did *not* have my spiritual act together. Being honest with these women and refusing to bolster the shield of perfection ushered in true comfort. They prayed for me and encouraged me. I was comforted by their acceptance of my troubled heart and their solidarity for that day's harshness. It was worth the risk of being real.

Everything worthwhile happens when we are free to be honest, free from the need to be perfect. And when we are free, we allow others to be free also. Toni Raiten-D'Antonio is a therapist who began using principles from the children's book *The Velveteen Rabbit* to assist her clients in processing their difficulties. The story is about a stuffed bunny that is insecure about his place in the nursery and what he considers his fatal flaws. Raiten-D'Antonio saw the bunny's transformation process as reflective of our own formative process, and she collected these concepts for her book *The Velveteen Principles: A Guide to Becoming Real*. Foundational to her strategy is helping people be honest about who they are so they can engage in loving, authentic, and healthy relationships. She explains: "People who demand perfection from themselves generally start to demand it from everyone else, too. [We treat people as if they] don't require our loving care, compassion and consideration. Like many characters in *The Velveteen Rabbit*, we may come to believe that only people who are shiny and modern have value."[12]

The habit of perfection robs us of intimacy with others, first by our inauthentic lives and second by our inability to show compassion for the needs of others. Only humility allows us to be real. Only from that real place can we step into the needs of others and extend the compassion and comfort of God.

How do we practice this new habit of humility to combat the drive for perfection? What's helped me is having a bunch of friends who truly know me—all the parts of me: the good, the bad, and the really ugly. There is no need to don a mask or feign perfection with them. Being known like this frees me to practice humility and put perfectionism to death. Being real invites others to be real too. In the light of truth, we can comfort each other as the wounded healers God has redeemed us to be. Together we can comfort each other in our weakness with the perfect comfort of God.

DISRUPTING THE STATUS QUO

Saying yes to compassion, trust, and humility is a way to say yes to God and learn to draw on his unending supply of comfort. Breaking free from small living is a matter of instituting new heart habits that disrupt the status quo where comfort has ruled for so long.

My dear friend Krista recently befriended Suba, a woman from India who speaks very little English. Krista willingly changed up her routine and left her comfort zone to help Suba run errands, take her to doctor's appointments, and try to communicate the love of Jesus while sipping many cups of chai. There were inconveniences. There were situations that felt unsafe. There were bumbles in communication. But God met Krista at every turn—filling her with his comfort so that she could practice compassion, trust, and humility. Just six weeks after Krista met her, Suba and her husband needed to return to India. Krista offered to drive them to the train station; all three wept at the parting.

Isn't that lovely? These are the memories that build a life worth living. When we buck the status quo to practice compassion, trust, and humility, we live free from serving self, free to serve others. And when we serve the least and the needy and the sorrowful, we need fully functioning hearts. That's our next stage in this comfort detox journey. For only love will compel us to lay down our lives for our brothers and sisters and be the comfort agents God has called us to be.

COMFORT CLEANSE

Step 15: Practicing Compassion

Choose a day. Today, even. Ask God for a divine appointment in which you can practice compassion toward someone in need of his comfort and compassion. Keep a journal handy and record how your day unfolds.

Step 16: Practicing Trust

Take time today to sit quietly with God and ask him to reveal his heart toward you. Note the words, phrases, or Scriptures that come to mind. Meditate on these words daily for the next week. Imagine what difference it would make in your life if you trusted God's heart, and ask God to make it real to you so you can make that truth real to others.

Step 17: Practicing Humility

Spend time with the Lord mulling over your place as the creature and God's place as Creator. Ask God to strengthen your dependence on him for comfort so that you can be humble toward others in need. Invest in authentic friendships that allow you to practice being the real you in every situation.

Engaged

*No one can help anyone without becoming involved,
without entering with his whole person into the painful
situation, without taking the risk of becoming hurt,
wounded or even destroyed in the process.*

HENRI NOUWEN,
THE WOUNDED HEALER

Here's the thing. Once we start practicing habits of compassion, trust, and humility, our daily lives will shift. Egomania will diminish as we loosen our grip on our days and begin to extend God's comfort to others. Our days will become the intersection where the Comforter meets a world of needs, through us.

Adjusting our daily choices to serve others is merely the first step. The second is choosing to engage our hearts. We have to choose to care. As this happens we will be confronted with harsh realities. Our world isn't short on sorrow. Seriously, sometimes I am amazed any of us lasts as long as we do! Acknowledging our pain and that of others is risky business. The very thing we were attempting to keep at arms' length will get too close for comfort (literally). Henri Nouwen affirms that if we are to be of any help to others, of any good to each other in our sorrows, we need to enter with our "whole person into the painful situation."[1] Entering in full is the only way we can be a conduit of God's comfort.

Being involved in the sorrows of others means saying no to acedia, the old habit we practiced putting off in chapter three. It's time to replace it with a new, life-giving habit. We must practice saying yes to the risk of becoming involved. Practicing engagement is the way we become the comfort agents—the wounded healers—God intends us to be. We've got to be all in. We've got to feel all the feels we've been trying to push away.

CAN YOU FEEL IT?

I've been reading historical biographies on our country's founders the past few years. I love the history and artifacts, the peek into daily life for people who lived several hundred years ago. Something especially curious is the smallness of community then as compared to today. It was not uncommon in the eighteenth century for people to have contact with just a few dozen people, including family members, over the course of their entire lives. Limited means for long-distance travel and communication were contributing factors.

Small social circles are rare today. We have access to wider communities through online platforms and affordable travel, easily increasing our connections from a few dozen people to hundreds and even thousands. Not only are we aware of our friends' lives, but we also know about people from around the world. Sadly, bad news travels faster than good, so we are clobbered with life's plights from our closest loved ones to strangers in countries we've never even heard of.

Access to knowledge like this is almost more than we can bear, which is why acedia is so very appealing to me. I can tell where acedia has made my heart tough like Teflon: where it refuses to feel. The Shredding made me aware of my disengagement habit, and since then I've had plenty of circumstances in which to practice the opposite response.

Some time ago I was in the midst of reviewing a typical day's news scroll, catching up on Facebook happenings (or perhaps indulging in some distraction from writing), when a post caught my eye. Some people I know mainly via the Internet had just received heart-wrenching news about their baby due in just a few months. The post was a call for prayer; there were major developmental complications with the new life growing in her womb. Tests showed severe physical deformities. Doctors were predicting life-inhibiting—if not life-threatening—health complications as a result. The parents-to-be were told to prepare for the worst. Even the best-case scenario for their baby would include years of surgeries and round-the-clock medical assistance. I read the update several times; my heart sank for them and for the baby.

Then I had one of those time-stopping episodes where I could sense the Spirit urging me to wait rather than scroll along. I didn't know why, but I knew I needed to take in this news rather than push it aside. Honestly, I didn't want to linger in it. I didn't want to feel the fear, disappointment, and frustration. So I threw out all sorts of commonsense arguments to the Lord: *I've never met them in person—they have family and friends, so why would they need me to engage? I don't live anywhere near them—so I could not help in person anyhow. I have people right here I should be helping—why exert energy for people I hardly know?*

Round and round I went, tossing up one excuse after another, each one flimsier than the last. Finally I stopped my arguing and asked God what exactly he wanted from me. *Choose to care* is what I heard. I stared at my computer screen, reading the news again. *Choose to care.* If I cared, I would not run from the pain. If I cared, I would engage rather than run away. If I cared, I would keep watch in this sorrow, just as Jesus asked his friends to do in Gethsemane. *Could you not watch with me one hour?*

The longer I lingered, the more I felt the weight: this news was reality for real people. I could tell it had gotten beyond my Teflon coating because my heart was feeling something. Acknowledging this was real engaged my heart, and soon I was sobbing out prayers for this couple and their baby. I stayed with them in their sorrow, before the throne of grace. For weeks afterward, I kept watch with them whenever the Spirit prompted me to pray. It didn't matter that I hardly knew them—God did, and his heart was heavy for his people. God was grieving over this brokenness, and he was asking me to keep watch with him in this sorrow. It didn't matter that I wasn't helping in person; praying is the ultimate act of faith as we trust God hears us and is moved by our engagement. It didn't matter that I have people right here to tend to—because the more I keep watch with Jesus, the more my heart learns this new habit of engagement for the benefit of everyone.

Practicing the habit of engagement for these Internet friends required me to go all in. It required me to bear another's burden—even of people I don't really know. It cost me emotional comfort, time, tears. But in the process of caring, my heart came alive in places I didn't even know were frozen and numb. Choosing to engage in another's sorrows brought life to my heart, proving that pain wasn't as pointless as I had thought.

MAKING PEACE WITH PAIN

Dr. Paul Brand discovered a world-altering truth about pain in his groundbreaking medical research with leprosy patients in the 1950s. Leprosy's presence was visible among the suffering as they lost fingers, toes, ears, and more. But no one could determine why leprosy had this effect on its victims. Eventually Dr. Brand's research revealed that leprosy was not randomly sloughing off body parts. Rather, leprosy deadened the presence of pain in the body. Lepers were moving through life with no ability to discern hot or cold, soft or hard, blunt or sharp. The result? People could not feel that they were injuring themselves. As those injuries went undetected, infection would set in, causing permanent damage and loss of body parts.

Dr. Brand's research proves that pain serves a significant purpose. People without pain sensors are destined to even greater suffering. All this is detailed in Dr. Brand's book *The Gift of Pain*. The title drew me in because it was the opposite of what I had always thought. Physical pain is actually God's built-in mechanism alerting us to danger or to something in need of attention.[2]

Although Dr. Brand's research focused on the physical experience of pain, I believe the same is true for emotional pain. When we experience emotional pain, it is God's built-in mechanism alerting us to something in need of care and attention. If we ignore that pain, if we refuse to come out of our acedia fog, we become emotionally leprous. Our hearts grow incapable of sensing heartache, and deformity soon follows. Practicing the habit of caring and engagement is actually vital to our emotional health.

Emotions—those of both joy and pain—were given to us by God for a reason. He meant for us to feel. When we refuse to engage, emotional leprosy deforms God's design. We become stunted and impaired, unable to function properly. Consider this from G. Walter Hansen's article "The Emotions of Jesus":

Jesus reveals what it means to be fully human and made in the image of God. His emotions reflect the image of God without any deficiency or distortion. When we compare our own emotional lives to his, we become aware of our need for a transformation of our emotions so that we can be fully human, as he is.[3]

Reading the Gospel accounts, I am amazed by how freely Jesus expressed the full range of his emotions. He was compassionate, loving, zealous, sorrowful, angry, surprised, joyful, indignant, and grieved. Jesus is the most fully alive human, the only one free from sin's distortions on the heart and soul. Practicing the habit of acedia numbs us, making us *less* human, less Christlike. We may run from pain to a false comfort, but it will only bring an increasing shadow of death. God's intention for us in Christ is to become more and more alive, more and more like Jesus. But how does that happen? We walk in his footsteps. We choose to care. We move toward people in need. How Jesus responded to pain is our example. His heart was fully functioning, without deformity. We must move toward Jesus by choosing to engage with our whole heart.

Hansen continues, "Paul tells the Corinthians that as Christians gaze upon the glory of the Lord, 'with unveiled faces,' we 'are being transformed into his likeness with ever-increasing glory' (2 Cor. 3:18, NIV). The apostle is suggesting that looking intently on the Lord will bring about a metamorphosis into Christ's image by the Spirit."[4] I love the idea of transformation and ever-increasing glory. Until pain hits. Then acedia sounds pretty good again! Old habits die hard, don't they? But each time we encounter pain, we have the opportunity to practice. With each pass we are learning something more about bringing our hearts to life and avoiding those deep holes in the road that lead to death. Choosing to engage with the pain of the world is exactly what Jesus did, and we are to follow him down that road of suffering, trusting the Comforter's promise to meet our needs so we can then pass along his comfort to others.

A NEW HIDING PLACE

Choosing to feel and acknowledge pain isn't always welcome, even in Christian circles. I have heard the argument that Christians need to just put on a happy face. Sadly, stories of mishandled pain are all too common. I once attended a short-term Bible study with women I didn't know very well. Most of them were older than me, so I automatically took the role of learner, deferring to their wisdom. One day as we were discussing a passage, one woman broke down sobbing, hardly able to speak but trying to explain that something in her family was greatly amiss and upsetting to her. I didn't really know her, nor did I know her situation. Perhaps the leaders did. I expected that we would stop our discussion to minister to this need. Instead, the leader redirected our conversation back to the study guide questions.

I may have this scenario all wrong—maybe the leader was best friends with this woman and knew they would talk and pray specifically later. But I was flabbergasted. A woman is sobbing in pain, and we just keep on with our fill-in-the-blank workbook questions? It affirmed that this group was for Bible knowledge transfer, not for helping each other walk out those principles in our everyday realities. It reinforced the happy face ideal.

But I have realized that those who adhere to this happy face policy will one day find themselves completely disconnected from others—and Jesus. Timothy Keller addresses this in *Walking with God Through Pain and Suffering*:

> There is a tendency for us to say, "I am afraid of the grief, I am afraid of the sorrow. I don't want to feel that way. I want to rejoice in the Lord." But look at Jesus. He was perfect, right? And yet he goes around crying all the time. He is always weeping, a man of sorrows. Do you know why? Because he is *perfect*. Because when you are not all absorbed in yourself, you can feel the sadness of the world.[5]

Whether we disengage out of fear or false piety, the choice leads away from Jesus. Jesus, the Man of Sorrows, is our example, our role model. As God transforms us into the image of his Son, we should become known as a people of sorrows, people who feel deeply—and willingly. The fear of feeling the depths of the world's sorrows has just one answer: "There is no fear in love, but perfect love casts out fear" (1 Jn 4:18). Love is the answer here. Jesus was known as the Man of Sorrows because he *is* love embodied. We, the comforted, must be known as people of sorrows so that love becomes manifest in and through us.

Our old habit of hiding is upended when we practice the new habit of engagement. In that Bible study, we should have surrounded the grieving woman with arms of love and covered her situation in prayer. We should have refused to hide behind the agenda of the lesson and chosen the greater thing: we should have chosen to care. As Keller says, when we are not absorbed in ourselves and whatever agenda we have, we can choose to feel—we can choose to move toward the sorrows of others rather than hide from them. Jesus proclaimed this very thing, saying he "came to seek and to save the lost" (Lk 19:10). He set the example by seeking us in our hiding places—and we must do likewise.

> As God transforms us into the image of his Son, we should become known as a people of sorrows, people who feel deeply—and willingly.

Hiding is second nature to us. Adam and Eve hid from God in the garden, and so our tendency is to continue hiding today. There is an alternative, however. Instead of running away when the shadows of pain draw near, we can run to the greater shadow: the shadow of the cross. There we see the full weight of our pain and suffering coming to bear upon our Savior, who was willing to love us with a full heart, even though suffering would result. Only the shadow of the cross can provide the cover we need to follow Jesus in seeking others and engaging the world desperate for the Comforter.

Just as God called Adam and Eve to come out from their makeshift shelter, so he calls us and beckons us to what's real. He calls us to face reality—brokenness and all. And just as God did not leave Adam and Eve to face life physically naked, neither will he leave us emotionally naked when we are brave enough to emerge from acedia's cover. God covers us fully, hiding us in his Son, clothing us with himself. In Christ we are able to shake off acedia's fog and choose to care.

FREE TO FEEL

I'm a late adopter to The Lord of the Rings series written by J. R. R. Tolkien. I rather begrudgingly went with friends to see the first film adaptation, *The Fellowship of the Ring*. After that, though, I was hooked. I had to know what happened to my new friends—the hobbits Frodo and Sam, the wizard Gandalf, the ranger Strider— who were facing great danger and adventure. I devoured the entire book series before the second film was released.

By the end of the story, Frodo has endured an unbelievable journey filled with great hardship. He reminisces about the battles, the losses, the wounds, and the pain as he records them in a journal. The melancholy is palpable as he concludes, "There are some things that time cannot mend. Some hurts that go too deep . . . that have taken hold."[6]

Each of us knows this to be true. Some experiences have made deep impressions on us, permanently changing us. We have scars both physical and emotional as proof. Choosing to engage and to care is unappealing for this reason. Our scars haunt us. We know some hurts have taken hold of us and of others, and it feels easier to disengage. The Lord of the Rings series ends on a bittersweet note, one that echoes reality: some hurts cause scars that will last a lifetime.

I find solace in knowing that even Jesus has scars from his time on earth. He loved without hiding from the pain and suffering of others, and it resulted in a full measure of suffering. The crucifixion stakes bored holes in his hands and feet; the soldier's spear gashed his side. Jesus died from and was buried with those bloody wounds, and they remained even after he rose from the dead and was glorified. After some of the disciples saw Jesus alive once again, they told the rest. Thomas was skeptical: "But [Thomas] said to them,

'Unless I see in his hands the mark of the nails, and place my finger into the mark of the nails, and place my hand into his side, I will never believe.'...Then [Jesus] said to Thomas, 'Put your finger here, and see my hands; and put out your hand, and place it in my side. Do not disbelieve, but believe'" (Jn 20:25, 27).

Curious, isn't it, that Jesus was glorified scars and all? His wounds remind us of his sacrifice and love, empowering us to trust him. The same is true for the wounds we've gained in this life—they hold great power to remind, convict, heal, and comfort. Scars show that we have lived—that we know firsthand the realities of living in a broken world. Wounds connect us to one another in the human experience. All the places we've been hurt recommend us to one another for help and healing, becoming a common ground of sorts, in which we can bear one another's burdens because we're all in this together.

> **Wounds connect us to one another in the human experience.**

Our wounds are the channels by which the Comforter sends his present help to others. I found this to be true in my friendship with a woman I've met with almost weekly for a few years now. Laura and I started meeting due to our shared love for writing. As our friendship grew, our conversation shifted to writing as a means of entering into the wounds of others, of being present in the messy, painful places of life. What we discussed in theory soon turned practical: one of Laura's most cherished friendships began to disintegrate. Some scorched places in Laura's heart were screaming for comfort, and she had been leaning into this friendship for soothing. Her friend began to define some relational boundaries, which exposed Laura's old wound of abandonment from her childhood. Not only was Laura devastated by the shift in the friendship, but she also was forced to face childhood heartache. It was a double whammy.

The pain Laura was experiencing was familiar to me. Loss of friendship, place, familiarity, and security—I knew them firsthand due to the transient nature of my childhood. Although our wounds didn't match exactly, I had a sense of what Laura needed. (Well, mostly. She extended much grace to me in the moments I offered unhelpful or insensitive commentary!)

How did I practice engagement here? Laura says the most helpful thing I did was allow her to walk through the lengthy process of grief, fear, and disappointment without pushing her to simply get over it. Putting aside the need to fix Laura's pain was only possible because I knew that healing was God's job and being present was mine. To be present, I had to draw on God's comfort for me—only God could soothe my panic for Laura's pain, allowing me to be near instead of needing her to be fixed so we could both exit the place of suffering.

Frodo mused that some wounds have taken hold, that time cannot heal them. It's true. We do not know the measure of healing God has for us or anyone else in this life. The fear that I cannot fix another person's pain has fueled my disengagement in the past. But choosing to care means that I rightly embrace my role and allow God to do his. I am called to be God's comfort agent—choosing to keep company with the wounded. I am not called to heal or fix and make everything good as new. Only God can do that. It is his discretion, his responsibility. I am merely to be present with the suffering, remembering my own wounds and needs so that I can rightly respond to the wounds and needs I see in others.

Musician Christa Wells penned the song "Come Close Now," perfectly describing how difficult it is to be present to those who are hurting. If you've not heard it, you must give it a listen. These lyrics speak of our need to choose to care and to practice engagement when others are in pain:

I'm afraid of the space where you suffer
Where you sit in the smoke and the burn
I can't handle the choke or the danger
Of my own foolish, inadequate words
I'll be right outside if you need me
Right outside

What can I bring to your fire?
Shall I sing while the roof is coming down?
Can I hold you while the flames grow higher,
Shall I brave the heat and come close with you now?
Can I come close now?[7]

This song was on repeat for me as I wrote and processed these ideas about engagement. I reached out to Christa, and she shared these words:

> Most of us are born fixers, I think. We want to have answers and solutions and feel we are not helpless to relieve the suffering of our loved ones. We have the best intentions, but we wound each other by trying to make the pain go away overnight. Inadvertently we deprive each other of permission to feel the loss and grief properly. The sufferer feels pressured to put on a happy face and get past it. Ultimately, we need to be willing to be uncomfortable, because being with sad people can be super uncomfortable, but it's often in the dark seasons that we witness God's presence most vividly. We need to leave room for Him to do His thing instead of swooping in with a plan all the time.[8]

Isn't that true? We fear drawing close to the space of suffering. We fear the pain and our "own foolish, inadequate words." Fear, suffering, embarrassment, pain—all these are downright uncomfortable. That's why comfort tells us to back away, to keep a minimum safe distance.

Being an ambassador for Christ in the middle of brokenness takes a willingness to sit in the mystery for the long haul with someone whose hurts keep on hurting. It is a willingness to feel the full weight of what can't be explained away. The poet John Keats referred often to a literary concept called *negative capability*, the fact that some matters in writing (and in life) might have to be left unsolved, uncertain, unanswerable.[9] Some things will remain shrouded in mystery no matter how much we may strive for resolution and understanding.

If I am going to be present with others in their pain, I need to come to terms with the mysteries that God chooses not to resolve. I need to accept that negative capability is here, that it is possible some pains will not be resolved in this life. Faith is needed to trust in spite of what cannot be seen or healed or settled.

> **Am I willing to stand in faith, engaged in the brokenness that is shredding the world, and proclaim that God is still God, even when life doesn't change and hurts refuse to heal?**

Am I willing to stand in faith, engaged in the brokenness that is shredding the world, and proclaim that God is still God, even when life doesn't change and hurts refuse to heal?

This is an ambassador's duty: to rally trust for the one being represented, even when it seems he is absent and silent, even when the hurts won't be fixed. The bridge in "Come Close Now" reminds us that our answers fall flat in the face of suffering. Instead, we should come empty handed and raw, ready to sit in the grief and the mystery, however long it may take:

Lay down our plans
Lay down the sure-fire fix
Grief's gonna stay awhile
There is no cure for this

We watch for return
We speak what we've heard
We sit together, in the burn.[10]

Whatever plans or fixes we think we've mastered and packaged for suffering hearts are unnecessary. We have Jesus, and we have each other. We just need to sit together in the burn and wait for the miracle that follows the mystery.

With his strength, we can draw near to the fire of suffering and just be present for others. Brené Brown says, "Courage starts with showing up and letting ourselves be seen."[11] I agree—it is an act of bravery to put yourself in the middle of brokenness and be willing to be seen and be present. This is what it will take for us to put aside our need to fix and instead sit with others in the smoke and burn of suffering.

FREE TO GIVE

I wasn't really in the mood to talk. It was late, just past midnight (and way past my usual bedtime). My flight from New York to Colorado had gotten delayed several times that day, almost doubling my expected travel time. But the woman next to me on the airport tram didn't seem tired at all. She immediately initiated a conversation, unaware, of course, that I was not feeling up for small talk. My preference was to zone out and conserve the bit of energy I had remaining. My flesh was justifying my preference as reasonable; I was low on reserves and my comfort was worn thin.

Charles Duhigg says that when we are tired, it's easy to slip into old habits because it takes the least amount of energy.[12] Coasting on autopilot takes way less effort than choosing a new, unpracticed action. Although I was tired and susceptible to old habits of retreat, I was returning from a week of ministry in New York City, where I had been immersed in engagement. Those tender, new practices had me on alert on that late-night tram.

I quickly took my preferences and weariness to God, quietly begging for help to respond to this woman as Jesus would have. Although I still didn't feel like talking, I knew this was my old scarcity mentality trying to entice me away from trusting God with my needs. This woman had been placed before me, expressing her need for a listening ear, and I had a choice to make: I could trust God to meet my needs and then pass that comfort to her, or I could shut down and miss the chance to connect with another human being. By God's grace the former choice won. Kim and I had just twelve minutes to chat, but she immediately shared that she too was tired and weary. Her mom had died just two weeks before, and she was in the midst of divorcing her abusive husband, which included nasty court battles over their children. The more we talked, the more heartache spilled out. And because I'm a sympathetic crier, when she began to weep, I did too.

When the conversation began, I was worried about being engaged for twelve minutes. But with God's unending supply of compassion for Kim (and me), twelve minutes wasn't long enough. We continued talking all the way to the baggage claim. Kim thanked me for listening, and I promised I would pray for her, which unlocked a new flood of tears. After I shared with Kim the only hope I know, we hugged, then went our separate ways.

Jesus says that we can show our care for him by showing care to the least in this world. Kim was among the least that night. She was lonely, discouraged, and hopeless. Jesus wanted her to know that he cared about the loss of her mom, the loss of her marriage, the pain of a horrible divorce, and the fear for her children's well-being. I cannot help but think that God arranged our meeting on that late-night tram so he could demonstrate his compassion for her.

The divine appointment wasn't just for Kim. God wanted to meet me there too. He wanted me to practice leaning into his endless supply of comfort when I was so obviously spent. It's God's comfort that needs distributing, not mine. I am merely a conduit, an agent on assignment, the hands and feet of the Comforter to everyone in my sphere.

Trusting in God to meet my needs and those of others is necessary to dismantle the scarcity mentality that has become our autopilot thinking. In our own strength we will not know how to help or what to say. We will always be short on comfort to give when we are trusting ourselves. Learning to access God's comfort is key.

When people are going through rough emotional waters, scarcity mentality prompts us to give a little morsel of wisdom and send the suffering on their way. One platitude that particularly stirs my ire is "God doesn't give you more than you can handle." Although well-intentioned, this pseudo encouragement is a variation on the injunction to quit your grousing and pull yourself up by your own bootstraps. But here's the thing: if God only gives us what we can handle, then that means we don't even need God, because we've got it all covered. It means that God is handing out pain because he knows we're capable. I don't know about you, but that makes me feel even worse. It tells me I'm alone—God expects me to figure it out using the strength I've got. And it makes me doubt God's goodness, sending me straight back to scarcity mentality: I need to live from the comfort I've collected, and there likely isn't extra for anyone else.

Erin Davis counsels in her book *Connected*, "When others are messy, you can't . . . offer cheap words of comfort."[13] Cheap words cost us little in terms of opening our hearts to the hurting. But they perpetuate the lie that God has nothing valuable to offer, so it's better for everyone if that pain is stuffed down and forgotten. We don't have to shoo the needy away with empty platitudes, though. God has much to say and much to offer when we step into the mess and the pain and pass along God's comfort. We—the needy ones— can engage with others in need because we are empowered by God.

This is why Jesus said, "Blessed are the poor in spirit, for theirs is the kingdom of heaven" (Mt 5:3). At first read, it doesn't make sense that the poor would own the kingdom of heaven. But Jesus affirms they have access to it and all its supply precisely because they know their poverty and are forced in desperation to depend on God for everything. Those who know they are poor become rich because they are dependent; they know they have nothing apart from God.

Interestingly enough, cultivating an awareness of my great need is the first defense against scarcity mentality. Scarcity mentality creates panic within me, as I constantly assess my comfort reserves and try to ration them to cover all my needs. Reality forces me to remember that I am truly poor and needy. I have nothing; therefore, I need God, who has everything—and therefore, I am rich, with the kingdom of heaven at my disposal.

FEELING ALL THE FEELS

The world is desperate for hearts to be fully alive and engaged. Right where you are, your life intersects with countless people who need someone to come close in the hour of suffering. It could be a lonely neighbor, a homeless man, an angry teen, a stressed-out mom, a doubting saint, a searching soul. People in your midst need you to be brave enough to sit with them in their sorrow, to share the load by choosing to feel and choosing to trust God's promises.

The Comforter is near to help you be present with others and be his ambassador. Each time you take the risk and engage your heart, you will find God faithful, to you and to the world. Opening your heart changes everything—and as we'll see in chapter nine, it will even shift your heart's desires and your life pursuits. Choosing to engage is a beautiful habit that mirrors the heart of the God who left heaven to come close. And now we get to follow his lead.

COMFORT CLEANSE

Step 18: Practicing Engagement

Visit erinstraza.com/comfort-detox and follow the link to listen to the song "Come Close Now" by Christa Wells.

Whose fire of sorrow can you be near this week?

Step 19: Practicing Abundance

Find fifteen to twenty minutes and a quiet spot. Grab a piece of paper and some pens. Ask the Comforter to remind you of the riches of your inheritance in Christ—all that you have access to because of Jesus. Begin to write down the words and phrases that come to mind, filling the page with words in a variety of colors, letter styles, and sizes. Meditate on God's abundance promised to you.

- 9 -

Captivated

*We were created to be part of
something so big, so glorious, so far beyond
the ordinary that it would totally change the way
we approach every ordinary thing in our lives.*

PAUL DAVID TRIPP, *A QUEST FOR MORE*

Early on, The Question upset me because I thought it had come to mock and attack. The *what-am-I-doing* query had a greater purpose, however. It was the gateway to an even deeper question, one echoing in every heart—one every courageous heart dares to entertain. It's the premise of everything Paul David Tripp addresses in *A Quest for More*. It's a simple two-word question that cracks open all hope: *What if?*

What if is the fodder of dreams and vision and ambition. In regard to our comfort detox journey, *What if* is the question we sidestep with an easy-to-consume vice when our hearts scream for comfort. But as we have put off the old self-soothing ways and put on the new life-giving ones, we find courage and dare to dream our what ifs.

Ultimately, we long to know that life is greater than hopping from one self-soothing gala to another. We want something more.

What if we were created to be part of something big? What if we were meant for something far beyond the ordinary? What if we were made for something glorious? We hope beyond hope this could be true. *A Quest for More* speaks to the longing that hangs about the edges of our lives and pushes us to seek meaning from our days.

We desire meaning in life precisely because we were designed that way. God created us for something meaning*ful*. Our hearts automatically hum to a tune of transcendence that's familiar yet foreign, like something from a dream we can't quite remember. That music has been woven into us by our Creator, and every time we catch a note of it on the wind, our hearts burn with desire for a life that is more than ordinary. The Question comes to shake us out of old habits and old ways, to wake us up to the captivating truth: we were made on purpose, for a purpose.

We were made for God's kingdom—which is why those old ways of comfort never satisfied. Now we must pick up the new habits of a new life. Those old ways aren't worth it anyhow when we have kingdom life to live! Therein we find the life we've been looking for, the one The Question has been leading us to all along. God's kingdom is where transcendence is found, and it's more than anything we can ask or imagine (Eph 3:20). God means to make us his kingdom people. He means to captivate us unto himself.

TRUE CITIZENSHIP

On the last afternoon of my trip to India, our team stopped at a fabric market with hundreds of vendors selling sari panels, ready-made textiles, and fabrics by the yard. It was glorious! The zest of colors, patterns, and textures were a feast for Western eyes that see black as chic. We wandered the market with our national guides, who helped us understand prices and purchase procedures.

I found something to buy, but credit card purchases were processed at the main desk and would take some time. It was decided that Veer, one of the guides, would stay with me while the rest of the team continued browsing. Veer and I stepped to the side of the booth and waited. With so many shoppers around, at first I didn't notice the man who had come up on our left. But he caught our attention pretty quickly when he pulled out a camera and started taking photographs of me. Veer's reaction was immediate—and forceful. His voice rose in anger and in a flash he was moving toward the photographer, who turned to run. Veer ran after him, shouting, leaving me at the booth alone. I had no idea what was going on.

Within ten minutes or so Veer returned, apologizing profusely for leaving me there. He explained that because Americans are highly respected in India, our presence at the market was a win. It's most likely that this photographer wanted to use the photos in promotional pieces to draw more shoppers. But Veer was having none of that; he chased the photographer down, grabbed the camera, and deleted the photos. (As far as I know, I am not the face of an Indian fabric market.)

Our team discussed the ordeal later, and our guides explained the value Indians place on having American connections. Being an American or being an Indian who knows English or who has studied or worked in the United States greatly enhances your social status. Such fuss over my nationality was new to me. I'm grateful to be an American, of course. But because I've always been one, it's second nature to me. I don't think about it much. It's just a fact.

As a Christian, I am also a citizen of heaven. And like my US citizenship, because I've held this privilege for twenty-five-plus years, it's second nature to me. It's a fact that I appreciate but rarely ponder.

In regard to this comfort detox journey, knowing my true citizenship is vital. If I merely see myself as a US citizen, a resident of earth, I will set my aim on gaining as much comfort as this world has to offer. And in so doing I will miss out on the riches of my inheritance in the kingdom of God.

Knowing who God says we are drastically influences the way we live. It doesn't take much digging in the Scriptures to find the benefits of heavenly citizenship. In Colossians we learn that we've been miraculously brought into a new kingdom: "The Father . . . has delivered us from the domain of darkness and transferred us to the kingdom of his beloved Son, in whom we have redemption, the forgiveness of sins" (Col 1:12-14). This means we no longer have to live by the ways of the old kingdom—the one driven by consumerism and materialism. We've been delivered from the false comforts of possessions and wealth and gain. We are free.

As part of this new kingdom, we now have a new identity. We are not who we used to be. Paul explains it like this in his letter to the Galatians: "I have been crucified with Christ. It is no longer I who live, but Christ who lives in me. And the life I now live in the flesh I live by faith in the Son of God, who loved me and gave himself for me" (Gal 2:20). In addition, God has blessed us with every spiritual blessing, chosen us before the world began, loved us, predestined us for adoption, redeemed us, forgiven us, lavished his grace on us, given us an inheritance, and sealed us with his Spirit—all this is stated in Paul's letter to the Ephesians (1:3-14). With this new identity, our worth is no longer tied to old kingdom values such as status, wealth, and personal fulfillment. We are free.

Along with a new kingdom and a new identity, we also have new purpose: "You shall love the Lord your God with all your heart and with all your soul and with all your mind. This is the great and first commandment. And a second is like it: You shall love your neighbor as yourself. On these two commandments depend all the Law and the Prophets" (Mt 22:37-40). The old kingdom had turned us into fearful, self-centered hoarders, but God has released us to live in love toward him and others—and ourselves. We are free, indeed.

A new kingdom. A new identity. A new purpose. These benefits are bestowed on every citizen of heaven. This freedom allows us to practice our allegiance to our new King and his kingdom by putting on the mindset and behaviors befitting our new home, identity, and calling.

Practicing our true citizenship happens in a multitude of ways. It's when we put the needs of others ahead of our own. It's when we seek to advance others ahead of ourselves. It's when we look for ways to extend comfort to the least, even when, by old-kingdom standards, it is a loss to us. All these things subvert the old kingdom and say no to false comfort. All these things point to a trust in God's kingdom to satisfy our deepest needs and to completely comfort us.

> **A new kingdom. A new identity. A new purpose. These benefits are bestowed on every citizen of heaven.**

The American dream has taught us to trust in the world's kingdom to comfort and satisfy. We exploit the old kingdom by using our work to build up mini-kingdoms of wealth, power, and prestige. But in God's kingdom, our work—whether it's in business, construction, education, transportation, or food service—becomes our way to build God's kingdom and share his comfort with those in need. The gospel captivates us with God's sure promises to provide everything we need for life and godliness, every spiritual blessing we could ever require. And because his supply never runs dry, we can use what we have been given to comfort others and invite them to become citizens of heaven too.

When we live in the reality that God's kingdom is already ours, we don't want anyone else to miss out. That's why the American dream is so destructive—we get consumed by its pseudo comforts and we forget that other people are on the outside. David Platt warns against this sort of life: "While Christians choose to spend their lives fulfilling the American dream instead of giving their lives to proclaiming the kingdom of God, literally billions in need of the Gospel remain in the dark."[1]

Ultimately, our true citizenship is about building God's kingdom—not our own. It involves displacing ourselves from center stage, because this story isn't about us. We are not the main character—Jesus is. We certainly have important parts to play, but we cannot do so by trying to steal the show. Writer Jason Moreland explains it like this:

> The Bible is about Christ and His amazing deeds. . . . If Christ is the hero, then we are not. We are not strong, he is. We are not awesome, he is. We are not worthy, he is. And if you live in a culture that values autonomy and power as much as America's does, then such thoughts run completely counter to some of the fundamental assumptions under which we live.[2]

Living to make Jesus the hero is contrary to the values in our birth country. We may have detoxed from the habits of autonomy, power, greed, consumption, and materialism, but those patterns run deep. God will need to strip away the invisible, self-centered norms of our old country and instill the norms of the new. He will need to teach us new ways of living that place him at stage center. This is why we must practice our true citizenship. We have much to learn.

Pastor Timothy Keller places all these changes under the umbrella of Christian discipleship. This is the lifelong process in which three remarkable things happen. First, a disciple sets a new priority for life: to follow Jesus wherever he leads. Second, a disciple loses herself to find a whole new identity. Third, a disciple is transformed by a radical experience with the mercy, grace, and love of Jesus. Keller stresses that our priorities and identity will never be altered without our hearts first being transformed by the amazing mercy of Jesus.[3]

In our comfort detox journey we've touched on all three of these discipleship markers. First, we have a new priority for life, and it doesn't include everyday egomania or the American dream or acedia. We are on assignment to pass along God's comfort to anyone in need. Second, we must lose ourselves to find a whole new identity, because true citizens cannot operate out of scarcity mentality or obsessive self-improvement. We are now citizens of heaven, sent by the Most High King to keep watch with those in sorrow. And third, we must be transformed by the mercy of God, because our old vices, addictions, and habits no longer align with our new lives.

Who are we, really? We are the comforted of God, called to keep watch with others in their sorrow, thereby being God's hands and feet of mercy to the least in the world as we extend his comfort to anyone in need. It's a high calling, one that captivates both heart and soul.

A PLACE IN THE PALACE

Learning to live everyday life as a disciple of Jesus—as a true citizen of God's kingdom—doesn't render our earthly citizenship void. In fact, being a good heavenly citizen makes us better earthly ones. Every benefit we have in being US citizens can be repurposed and rededicated for God's kingdom. So there's no need to feel guilty for whatever state of wealth you find yourself in. Being a good heavenly citizen may require you to become a poor US citizen (that's between you and the Lord), but that's not what kingdom citizenship is truly about. It's about dedicating everything you have, tangible and intangible, for the good of others. Francis Chan says, "It is true that God may have called you to be exactly where you are. But, it is absolutely vital to grasp that he didn't call you there so you could settle in and live your life in comfort and superficial peace."[4]

The benefits and privileges I enjoy as both a US citizen and a heavenly one are immense. They're not just material things—they're resources, opportunities, freedom, education, access, and more. And to whom much is given, of them much is required (see Lk 12:25-48). The blessings I have are not intended to dead-end here in my life but to be passed along, reinvested, and recycled for the good of others. Because of Jesus, I am now on assignment as an agent of comfort, one who receives God's love and mercy to then deliver it to anyone in need.

That takes work. It takes eyes up, ears open, and heart soft to engage the world around me. It takes me being more consumed with the needs of others than with my own. It takes intentionality to keep the blessings moving. I need a revolving-door mentality—comfort comes in but is spun right back out again before I assume full possession of it.

The Valley of Vision, a collection of prayers and devotions, states it like this: "Have mercy on me, for I have ungratefully received thy benefits, little improved my privileges."[5] That phrase crushes me: "I have . . . little improved my privileges." *Ugh*. So true. I have been given much, and most of it I have squandered on my own comfort and spent on my own pleasure. Awareness that I am in the wealthiest 1 percent in the world helps to put it in perspective. Most of what I want to buy is in the extra and better category. Recognizing the blessed life US citizens have been handed turns me outward toward the needs of others. I desperately need to practice a new life-giving habit that makes the most of what God has entrusted to me.

When my sister's kids were younger and learning to read, I wanted to be part of that process. Reading and books have played a tremendous role in my life—shaping, teaching, stretching, and entertaining me. In hope that my niece and nephews would develop a love for reading, just like their mom and aunt, I established a weekly reading time, taking one child a week for an hour of reading at a local coffee shop. These outings may have also included a cookie and a whipped-cream-and-chocolate-sauce-drizzled hot cocoa. (Because I'm the Aunt.) I enjoyed this time with my niece and nephews immensely. As kids are wont to do, however, they grew up. Eventually reading time was not needed.

Some time after this, my church announced it was organizing tutoring sessions for one of our local elementary schools. Volunteers were needed to help first graders improve their reading scores. There was no doubt I needed to sign up. I was placed with two girls, and we began meeting each week to review flashcards, play word games, and read books. It was lively and challenging and joyful. At the end of the term, I gave each girl a book with a note encouraging them to keep reading and affirming how much I enjoyed spending time with them.

The differences are sobering between these two sets of kids in terms of need and opportunity. My sister's kids receive a good deal of attention and help from their parents, grandparents, aunts and uncles, and coaches and teachers. We all lovingly and willingly invest in them, wanting to ensure every opportunity is open to them for a bright future.

But those two girls I tutored? The supervising teacher told me the extra time I spent was likely the best attentive time the girls would receive from an adult all week. They had challenges at home that greatly hindered their ability to learn and put them at a deficit emotionally and mentally. I later learned that one of the girls refused to put her new book down the rest of the school day; she was hugging it because it was the only book she owned. I cannot begin to tell of the tears I have cried and the prayers I have prayed over this.

Disparities in this life aren't new. I get that. Even Jesus said the poor would always be with us (Mk 14:7). But the deficits hurt more when they affect your own people—the loved ones you are intimately involved with and connected to. This is exactly why we must continue putting off the habits that keep our lives self-focused and self-involved. We must put on habits that draw us into the gaps so that the least of the world become "our people." Jesus did this by taking on our damaged flesh and walking among us. Likewise, we must identify that closely with the least in the world.

Some people are doing this literally by moving into lower-income neighborhoods to serve with their everyday lives. Some are downsizing their lifestyle to have more resources to give away. Some are volunteering at homeless shelters or community ministries. However God calls each one of us to do so, we must follow Jesus' example. He opened his daily life to others in compassion, trust, and humility. He allowed his heart to engage with the pain others were enduring. He remembered his kingdom purpose.

> **We must put on habits that draw us into the gaps so that the least of the world become "our people."**

Soon after my term at the elementary school ended, I was reading Timothy Keller's *Every Good Endeavor*. In it Keller speaks of using your gifts, talents, and vocation to build God's kingdom right where you are, whether you are a scientist, engineer, hair stylist, musician, pastor, barista, or whatever. Whatever we do, wherever we are, we are to use it to help others flourish. Keller likens it to the place of influence gained by Esther, the queen whose life is detailed in the Old Testament book bearing her name. Esther was in the palace by providence: the king chose her as his queen because of her beauty and character, and she was given a position of power she had never expected. When a plot arose to destroy all the Jewish people in the land, Esther's life was in danger—the king was not aware that Esther was Jewish too. Esther's cousin implored her to make a case with the king to rescue them all—a case only she could make because she was in the palace, in a place of power. Keller shares:

> I remember years ago hearing a Hispanic pastor preaching on the book of Esther. Many of his older church members had been immigrants and had little money or clout, but many of the younger generation had gone to college and had become professionals. The preacher told them that even though they didn't see it, they were "in the palace." They had more financial and cultural capital than they realized. And, he said in no uncertain terms, many of them were using that capital to feather their own nests and move ahead in their own careers rather than leveraging it for others.[6]

Yes. This is it exactly. Just as Esther was in the palace by providence, so are we. God has placed us in positions of power and influence, some of which we are completely unaware of. Just as Esther's cousin nudged her to step into her God-given position of influence, so too does the Spirit nudge us today. We can leverage what we have for the good of others. Especially here in the United States—and here in the church—we have money, clout, education, time, opportunities, voices, respect, influence, connections, talents, and resources. We are modern-day Esthers. We have a place in the palace, a seat at the table of influence. There is much good we can do if we practice the habit of leveraging that influence to benefit others rather than feathering our own nests, so to speak.

It's important to grasp the danger Esther faced in pleading to the king. She was tossing in her lot with her people; to use her place of influence, she was risking her very life. That's a challenge to me, for my sacrifices to date have not put me in danger. But that doesn't mean God will not require this.

If we are to use our influence to the full, some things must die. But that death will give way to true life, for ourselves and others, as we practice living as God's comfort agents. We must look for ways to leverage—to spend, invest, pour out—what we have been given. That includes our clout, our opportunities, and our resources. We need to sow them in places currently lifeless and void, where people are desperate for God's comfort. We need to look for those who otherwise have no voice, no place, and no hope, and go there. The time I spent tutoring those two girls is an example of this. It was a simple act, but one that helped the girls test at their grade level. Did that change the trajectory of their education? I may never know. But God called me to that gap, that place of need, and I sowed the seeds of life that I had been given. And I trust those seeds will not return void.

There are plenty of other stories like this, of people leveraging their place in the palace for the good of others.

Simone is helping women transition out of the horrors of human trafficking. She has worked tirelessly to open Naomi's House, where women will be able to rebuild their lives and find hope and healing.

Sara and Mitchell opened their hearts and home to two girls from India. The girls now have the loving parents they've been longing for, as well as an extended family that is wild about them.

My mom knits hats and scarves—by the hundreds—for underprivileged kids. She hates the idea of kids walking to school in the cold because they cannot afford to bundle up.

Krista and Mark are coworkers who volunteer together for an hour every other Friday at the local mission. They take a van to the grocery store and pick up donated food for the mission's food bank.

I could go on and on. Every one of my friends is doing something remarkable to push back against the status quo. With each push, we practice the new habit of leveraging our place in the palace for the good of others, offsetting our old habit of over-reaping our lives for our own benefit. All these acts of service take time that could be spent serving self. All these take a willingness to say no to emotional distance. All these take a stance against the American dream. Author D. L. Mayfield calls this a life of downward mobility: "How can I turn the tables on a world, a system, that is meant to enslave and crush and oppress? I can start by giving up power, by choosing to live a simple, quiet life, or become a refugee in a new land, or stake my tent in a community of outcasts—I can start by embracing the freedom that failure in the empire brings."[7]

Our true citizenship in God's kingdom has freed us to say no to the world's empire. Instead we can serve, love, get low, trust God's promises, magnify someone else's voice, give up our status, donate time and money, go where God leads, refuse to worry about tomorrow, and get busy living the kingdom life. Even our small efforts shine as acts of rebellion in the face of vanity, paving the way out of the old kingdom and into the new.

Especially for those of us who are in God's kingdom, serving others is part of our new identity, our spiritual DNA—we serve because Jesus did and he calls us to be servants of all. Scripture admonishes that "as we have opportunity, let us do good to everyone, and especially to those who are of the household of faith" (Gal 6:10). And so we should do whatever we can to pass along God's comfort wherever we find a need for it among our brothers and sisters in Christ.

However, as author Jen Hatmaker urges, there is more. She calls us to use our status as modern-day Esthers to "step outside the tidy boundaries where you spend your time serving saved people and blessing the blessed."[8] God's comfort must go beyond our church walls to reach those who are desperate for true comfort. If we do not go to the least and the forgotten, the overlooked, the marginalized, the shunned, who will?

FOR MY SISTERS

From the first pages of this book, I pointed to the grief God must bear over the sorrow and brokenness that permeate this earth and every human heart. The pain is not just what is here today, but it is the pain from every day for every person in every nation ever since Adam and Eve were the first to rebel and set sin's consequences in motion. Who among us can comprehend the cumulative weight of that collective grief that God must bear?

Regardless of our inability to comprehend God's grief, we can come close to him in his sorrow and keep watch with him. We can open our hearts to bear that burden with him, as small a measure as it may be.

A large part God's grief is caused by the injustices women endure worldwide. Women face the horrors of abuse, marginalization, exploitation, and discrimination. I saw the hopelessness of that in India's red-light district, where it is estimated that girls born in the district have a 95 percent chance of becoming enslaved there themselves.[9] The system that enslaves mothers claims the daughters.

And then there are the Muslim women who are oppressed under the most extreme forms of Islam. Kate McCord shares her personal experience in her book *In the Land of Blue Burqas*. McCord lived in Afghanistan for five years; she recounts her conversations and insights into this culture that stands in stark contrast to ours. Life for women in that country is narrow and slim in comparison, with few gaining education or career or travel or freedom. The women live cloaked, either behind compound walls or under blue burqas.[10]

Compared to the women McCord worked with in Afghanistan, the women I met in the red-light districts of India, and other stories we've heard from around the world, I am overwhelmed by all that has been afforded women in the United States. We have freedom, voices, opportunities, and choices. We are among the most free and privileged women on earth. Women here have the freedom to live as they so choose: to get an education, drive vehicles, vote, hold positions of authority in business and government, voice our opinions, and use our wealth to move mountains of injustice.

Maybe this is why it's so bothersome that even here, in the land of freedom and liberty, things aren't perfect. Here in the United States women battle against sexism, the glass ceiling, pay discrimination, and biases of all sorts. Systemic injustices plague our country—our people, our brothers and sisters, our children. If things cannot be right here, where the atmosphere is most conducive, it's doubtful it can be right anywhere. And that is discouraging, to say the least.

Before giving in to hopelessness, however, I think we have to look to all that can be done rather than all that is unfair and undone. We have the chance to engage in a specific part of kingdom work precisely because we are women with "a place in the palace": we are daughters of the King as well as US citizens. We are among the most privileged people on the planet, and our womanhood grants us additional benefits. My friend Hannah Anderson believes that a woman's vulnerability in the world may make her more keenly aware of the vulnerability of others. It's the result of lived experience. Our ability as women to relate to the fear, isolation, hopelessness, and oppression experienced by women worldwide is a powerful force urging us to action. Could it be that God is nudging us to be his comfort agents to our sisters precisely because we can relate?

I think so. Our true citizenship and our place in the palace can be leveraged in unique ways to deliver God's comfort to women suffering within corrupt systems. We can use what we've been given to initiate tangible, permanent change.

For example, we can help our sisters worldwide by ensuring they receive some of the opportunities we cannot imagine living without. Education is one such investment that dramatically changes the course of a woman's life. It is estimated that for every additional year of schooling a girl receives, her future earning power increases by 20 to 25 percent. Considering that women invest 90 percent of their income into their families, as compared to 30 to 40 percent for men, it is worth our every effort to ensure girls receive a proper education.[11] This is something we as women can do for fellow women around the world. There are countless organizations facilitating better education for girls. We can research the options and pick one to support with our resources and to advocate for with our voices.

Although educational opportunities are commonplace here in the United States, systemic injustices affect the quality of that education for minorities and for those living in poverty-stricken areas. Lack of education fuels the generational cycles of despair, hopelessness, racism, poverty, lack of opportunity, unemployment, lack of dignity, and the like. But if we heed the call to keep watch with God in his sorrows, we also must enter into this suffering right here at home. To do so we must begin to engage and listen to those who are outside the palace of privilege. What would happen, for instance, if we listened to those who are marginalized because of their race? Consider this from Ekemini Uwan:

Now more than ever, I find myself contemplating the indignities we so often suffer in silence, the indignities that go unnoticed by those who inflict them and by those of us who experience them, because enduring varying degrees of indignities has become our way of life—it is the air we breathe. I have given much thought to the broad paintbrush the media uses to paint men and women in our community. Their color of choice: aggression, because to depict us as the multifaceted, dynamic image-bearers we are would humanize us and heap guilt upon the consciences of those who treat us as less than who God created us to be. The indignities we have suffered in our past and present seek to strip us of our God-given humanity, with the intent that we imbibe the dehumanizing messages spoon-fed to us. Lies from the pit of hell seek to exalt themselves above the knowledge of Christ and are meant to keep us bound, silent, and complacent. As image-bearers, we can do no such thing—silence is not an option.[12]

Will we remain deaf and silent in response to such a cry when our place in the palace can be leveraged to make a difference? We can serve one another by suffering with one another and choosing to lay down our lives so the kingdom grows ever wider. There are countless ways for this to happen—but as with every change, it begins with being aware and choosing to engage in some way.

Even within our neighborhoods much can be done. You could leverage your place in the palace and your true citizenship by extending comfort to those across the street or across town. Are you a Bible study leader? Perhaps you could offer a Bible study at your mission or shelter where hope is hard to find. Are you a hair stylist? Maybe you could offer discounted hair care to women in need. Are you a business owner? Maybe you could offer jobs to those recently released from prison. Whatever you do, however God has gifted you, that's where you can stand in the gap for others. That is where you can meet a world of need with the comfort God has so graciously given you.

CAPTIVATED BY THE KINGDOM

I see glimpses of the kingdom around me, in the lives of those I know. The flashes are glorious. But there is a greater glory to come. One day we will see Jesus face to face, and all our longings will be satisfied in full. All the comfort we've been searching for—by controlling our everyday lives, keeping emotional distance, pursuing self-actualization—will one day be fulfilled.

Until then, we live in this already/not yet limbo where we must practice heavenly habits and become the kingdom people God has redeemed us to be. We keep pressing on to the transcendence that frees us, just as Paul David Tripp explains: "[God's] grace cuts a hole in your self-built prison and invites you to step into something so huge, so significant that only one word in the Bible can adequately capture it. That word is *glory*."[13]

That glory is not our own but God's. He is the one to magnify. He is the reason to engage a world of need. And because his glory changes everything, we must be about his business. There is too much to do and too much brokenness in this world for any of God's people to sit idle, amused by life pursuits that benefit only ourselves.

There is too much to do and too much brokenness in this world for any of God's people to sit idle, amused by life pursuits that benefit only ourselves.

We have been redeemed at a price and have the joy of heavenly citizenship. We have the high honor and privilege of bearing God's image to the world. Why would we live small lives centered on ourselves when we have the opportunity to display God's love and mercy to a world desperate for help and hope?

Lest you feel a pressure to greatness, let me be clear: God is actively redeeming the world by his glorious grace. We, as recipients of grace and stewards of his comfort, are called to witness to this reality. Being God's comfort agent is a way of living your life.

In benediction, I leave you with these encouraging and calming words:

So here's what I want you to do, God helping you: Take your everyday, ordinary life—your sleeping, eating, going-to-work, and walking-around life—and place it before God as an offering. Embracing what God does for you is the best thing you can do for him. Don't become so well-adjusted to your culture that you fit into it without even thinking. Instead, fix your attention on God. You'll be changed from the inside out. Readily recognize what he wants from you, and quickly respond to it. Unlike the culture around you, always dragging you down to its level of immaturity, God brings the best out of you, develops well-formed maturity in you. (Rom 12:1-2 *The Message*)

COMFORT CLEANSE

Step 20: Practicing True Citizenship

Your true citizenship comes with glorious benefits! To help you ponder the beauty of your citizenship, visit erinstraza.com/comfort -detox and follow the link to watch the three-minute video "From Being Undocumented to Becoming a U.S. Citizen." Process your thoughts about citizenship and share them with your friends.

Step 21: Practicing Influence

Make a list of the places of influence God has entrusted to your management and care. Include anything connected to your home, family, work, community, interests, and so on. Ask God to show you how you can use these places for the benefit of others, and choose one action step you can take in the next month.

Parting Words

A New Kind of Normal

So here we are. We've journeyed all this way together, and now our time together, at least in this book, is coming to a close. You've read all about my struggle with comfort and my etched-in-stone habits. You've read about The Shredding and how The Question haunted me. You've read about my tentative attempts to step out of my comfort zone and live as God's comfort agent for a world in desperate need. As much as I desire that my words have been helpful or insightful for your own journey, more than that I pray my words have pointed you to hope. Not just a flimsy, wispy, dream of a thing, but a sure and certain truth rooted in the promises of God to be the comfort we need so we can in turn be the comforters he is pleased to send on assignment.

Because of this high calling upon God's people, I also hope my words have been the Spirit's prod in your life. I pray this work is one means he will use to set right the ways comfort has gotten skewed in your life. Once God begins that process, it will continue until you see him face to face. Until then, we will all be on the way, learning to wean our hearts from pseudo comforts, learning to give away the comfort we've gained wherever there is a lack, learning to keep watch with the sorrowful and to tend to the least.

The process ushers in a new kind of normal, one that is painful, at least in the beginning, as we cooperate with God to put aside the natural comforts we've depended on for way too long. Old habits may be hard to break, but new ones are well worth the work. Living in God's kingdom requires a new language, one the Spirit uses to communicate with us about things we weren't attuned to previously.

At this point in my comfort detox journey, my desire to be more in tune with the Spirit continues to grow. It's his voice I seek to hear above the false comforters that surround me. My life is still in progress—and in process. I haven't yet arrived to the sort of life where I am on assignment every moment, at the ready for whatever need may cross my path.

The normal I want is one that eschews convenience, safety, and perfection by embracing compassion, trust, and humility so that I'm a willing servant of the king.

The normal I want is one that enters into the pain of others by sitting in the burn with those who mourn so that I might extend the presence of God from my own scorched places.

The normal I want is one that gives up vain pursuits in order to expand the comfort of those who have very few comforts available to them, who wonder whether God can even hear their cries.

This is the normal I long for. I'm not there yet. But I'm further along than I was. This is progress. This is hope.

How will you continue to pursue a new kind of normal in your comfort detox journey? The old habits delivered a life that was confined, detached, and absorbed. The new habits will lead you to a life that's free, engaged, and captivated.

I pray your awareness has increased and your desire for more than the status quo has been stoked. I pray you are encouraged to pursue the Comforter so that you will become the comforted of God.

NEXT STEPS

Now that you've read all these words and considered how they might apply to you, I don't want you to lose momentum. So here are some ways you can incorporate these principles into your life in the weeks and months and years to come.

Go back to the Comfort Cleanse exercises provided at the end of each chapter. If you completed them as you read, review your answers and ask God to work a new normal into your daily living. If you haven't completed them, be sure to start processing them each week until you've worked through them all.

Schedule a monthly check-in to review your progress. Based on your personal assessment, develop a detox or training exercise for the month ahead to give your comfort zone another stretch.

Practice turning to the Spirit when your soul craves comfort. When your convenient, safe, and perfect life is being challenged, turn to the Comforter and ask him to help you serve others rather than self. When you are tempted to disengage and numb out from the emotional pain you encounter, turn to the Comforter and ask him to fill you to the full so you have something to give. When you find yourself entangled in self-centered pursuits, turn to the Comforter and ask him to give you a better dream.

Gather your fellow pilgrims and Esthers and dream what difference you can make together as God's comfort agents. Then do something, even one thing. This is the way forward.

REMEMBER JESUS AND LIVE FULLY

As we close the cover on comfort detox, may you go forward in hope, trusting that God is working and moving with every small victory. May you have joy in all that God is doing. May you be free from the guilt that you aren't being perfect at being uncomfortable for the sake of the gospel.[1] Jesus already did that for us, you know. He made himself nothing to comfort us in our sin by breaking its power and claim over us. He came down from heaven, put on our broken flesh, endured persecution, died on a cross, and conquered death and hell. I'd say he was uncomfortable enough for us all. We cannot add to his work, but we can commune with him in our choices to embrace all he bought for us. He made a way for us to experience true comfort. It would be a sad waste not to enjoy it.

May you become the agents of comfort God intends you to be.

Acknowledgments

Throughout these pages are echoes of my family, friends, writers, pastors, teachers, coworkers, and acquaintances. Countless people have invested in me, shaping my thoughts and words. However, there are hearts, minds, and hands that brought this particular book to fruition.

Top billing goes to my husband, Mike. He was God's comfort in the flesh as I wrote every word, wrestled with revisions, and cried in frustration. We shared the sacrifice; now we share in the joy!

God's comfort was tangible through dear friends who listened as I developed the notion of comfort addiction and then shared their lives as a proof test for the concepts: Krista; lodge ladies Dorothy, Janet, Kathleen; Sherry; Rebecca; Lissa (my beloved sister); Laura; Becky; Lisa and Wendy; Mastermind gals Merritt, Alysa, Michaela, Trina; and the editors, writers, and members at Christ and Pop Culture. Thanks for the coffee dates, honest feedback, emergency prayer coverage, surprise mail, and silly memes.

I cannot rave enough about the team at InterVarsity Press. Helen Lee and Ethan McCarthy provided expert editorial direction and honest criticism. The creative work of the marketing team (Lorraine, Lori, Alisse, Krista, Beth) made it possible for readers beyond my family and friends to discover my book. Thanks for working with this first-time author.

My greatest comfort in life and in death is God's rescue found in Christ alone. This book is all about his love and mercy for comfort addicts like me.

Notes

INTRODUCTION: WHY A DETOX?

[1]Charles Duhigg, *The Power of Habit: Why We Do What We Do in Life and Business* (New York, NY: Random House, 2012), 19.

[2]Ibid., 20.

[3]Thomas Chalmers, *The Expulsive Power of a New Affection* (Minneapolis: Curiosmith, 2012), 19.

[4]James Clear, "How Long Does It Actually Take to Form a New Habit? (Backed by Science)," *The Huffington Post*, June 10, 2014, www.huffingtonpost.com/james-clear/forming-new-habits_b_5104807.html.

[5]Eugene Peterson, *A Long Obedience in the Same Direction: Discipleship in an Instant Society* (Downers Grove, IL: InterVarsity Press, 2000), 17.

CHAPTER 1: A SEVERE MERCY

[1]Rakesh Kochhar, "A Global Middle Class Is More Promise Than Reality," Pew Research Center, July 8, 2015, www.pewglobal.org/2015/07/08/a-global-middle-class-is-more-promise-than-reality.

[2]According to the Half the Sky Movement there are 2 to 3 million women and girls enslaved in India; "Forced Prostitution," accessed June 20, 2016, www.halftheskymovement.org/issues/forced-prostitution. According to the Coalition Against Trafficking in Women the number of prostitutes in India is about 7.9 million; "Facts and Statistics," Coalition Against Trafficking in Women—Asia Pacific, accessed June 20, 2016, https://catwap.wordpress.com/programs/research-documentation-publications/facts-and-statistics.

[3]Sheldon Vanauken, *A Severe Mercy* (New York: HarperCollins, 1977).

[4]A. W. Tozer, *A Disruptive Faith: Expect God to Interrupt Your Life* (Ventura, CA: Regal, 2011), 47.

CHAPTER 2: CONFINED

[1]Christopher Booker, *The Seven Basic Plots: Why We Tell Stories* (London: Continuum, 2004), 231-32.

[2]A. W. Tozer, *A Disruptive Faith: Expect God to Interrupt Your Life* (Ventura, CA: Regal, 2011), 73.

[3]Charles Duhigg, *The Power of Habit: Why We Do What We Do in Life and Business* (New York: Random House, 2012), 19-21.

[4]Tim Challies, "Spying Out the Land," Challies.com, October 8, 2012, www .challies.com/articles/spying-out-the-land.

CHAPTER 3: DETACHED

[1]Paul David Tripp, *A Quest for More: Living for Something Bigger Than You* (Greensboro, NC: New Growth Press, 2008), 63.

[2]Erin Straza, *The Story Guide Primer* (Bloomington, IL: Spread Truth Publishing, 2013), 29.

[3]Kathleen Norris, *Acedia and Me: A Marriage, Monks, and a Writer's Life* (New York: Riverhead Books, 2008), 3-4.

[4]Ibid., 37.

[5]Brené Brown, *Daring Greatly: How the Courage to Be Vulnerable Transforms the Way We Live, Love, Parent, and Lead* (New York: Gotham Books, 2012), 137.

[6]Ibid., 26.

[7]Ibid., 2.

[8]"The Breaking Point" (episode 7), *Band of Brothers*, produced by Steven Spielberg and Tom Hanks (United States: HBO, 2001).

[9]C. S. Lewis, *The Four Loves* (New York: Harcourt, Brace, 1960), 121.

CHAPTER 4: ABSORBED

[1]"The Declaration of Independence: A Transcription," National Archives and Records Administration, www.archives.gov/exhibits/charters/decla ration_transcript.html.

[2]James Truslow Adams, *The Epic of America* (Boston: Little, Brown, and Company, 1931), xvi.

[3]Chris Arnade, "Who Still Believes in the American Dream?," *The Atlantic*, September 23, 2015, www.theatlantic.com/business/archive/2015/09/amer ican-dreams-portraits/405907.

[4]Note to Ecclesiastes 1:2, The Holy Bible, English Standard Version (ESV) (Wheaton, IL: Crossway Books, 2011).

[5]A. W. Tozer, *The Pursuit of God* (Harrisburg, PA: Christian Publications, 1948), 112.

[6]Richard Stearns, *The Hole in Our Gospel* (Nashville, TN: Thomas Nelson, 2009), 120-24.

[7]Ibid.

[8]Anat Shenker-Osorio, "Why Americans All Believe They Are 'Middle Class'," *The Atlantic*, August 1, 2013, www.theatlantic.com/politics/archive/2013/08/why-americans-all-believe-they-are-middle-class/278240.

[9]Tom Stafford, "Drug Addiction: The Complex Truth," BBC, September 10, 2013, www.bbc.com/future/story/20130910-drug-addiction-the-complex-truth.

CHAPTER 5: THE COMFORTER

[1]A. W. Tozer, *The Pursuit of God* (Harrisburg, PA: Christian Publications, 1948), 7.

[2]Ibid., 97.

[3]Richard J. Foster, *Celebration of Discipline* (London: Hodder & Stoughton, 1989), 121.

[4]Portia Nelson, *There's a Hole in My Sidewalk: The Romance of Self-Discovery* (Hillsboro, OR: Beyond Words, 1993).

[5]Eugene Peterson, *A Long Obedience in the Same Direction: Discipleship in an Instant Society* (Downers Grove, IL: InterVarsity Press, 2000), 17.

[6]Henri J. M. Nouwen, *The Way of the Heart: Desert Spirituality and Contemporary Ministry* (New York: Random House, 1981), 21.

CHAPTER 6: THE COMFORTED

[1]Chimamanda Ngozi Adichie, "The Danger of a Single Story," TEDGlobal, July 2009, description at Ted.com, www.ted.com/talks/chimamanda_adichie_the_danger_of_a_single_story?language=en.

[2]"Narcissus," Encyclopedia Britannica Online, 2015, www.britannica.com/topic/Narcissus-Greek-mythology.

[3]Quoted in David G. McCullough, *John Adams* (New York: Simon & Schuster, 2002), 207-8.

[4]J. R. Vassar, *Glory Hunger: God, the Gospel, and Our Quest for Something More* (Wheaton, IL: Crossway, 2015), 22.

[5] David Platt, *Counter Culture: A Compassionate Call to Counter Culture in a World of Poverty, Same-Sex Marriage, Racism, Sex Slavery, Immigration, Persecution, Abortion, Orphans, and Pornography* (Carol Stream, IL: Tyndale House Publishers, 2015), xv.

[6] Matthew Henry, *Concise Commentary on the Bible*, available at BibleGateway, www.biblegateway.com/resources/matthew-henry/2Cor.1.3-2Cor.1.6.

[7] Michael Horton, *Christless Christianity: The Alternative Gospel of the American Church* (Grand Rapids: Baker Books, 2008), 118.

[8] Henri J. M. Nouwen, *The Wounded Healer: Ministry in Contemporary Society* (New York: Doubleday, 1979), 88.

CHAPTER 7: FREE

[1] Paul David Tripp, *A Quest for More: Living for Something Bigger Than You* (Greensboro, NC: New Growth Press, 2008), 16.

[2] See articles by Susan Cain and contributors at Quiet Revolution, www.quietrev.com.

[3] Judith Viorst, *Alexander and the Terrible, Horrible, No Good, Very Bad Day* (New York: Atheneum, 1975).

[4] Tim Challies, *Do More Better* (Minneapolis: Cruciform Press, 2015), 95.

[5] "One in Three Road Accidents Happen a Mile from Home, Survey Says," *The Telegraph*, August 13, 2009, www.telegraph.co.uk/motoring/news/6018081/One-in-three-road-accidents-happen-a-mile-from-home-survey-says.html.

[6] Corrie ten Boom, *The Hiding Place* (Washington Depot, CT: Chosen Books, 1971), 84.

[7] Joel Houston, Matt Crocker, and Salomon Lighthelm, "Oceans," from the Hillsong United album *Zion*, © 2013 Hillsong Music Australia under exclusive license to Capitol CMG Label Group/Sparrow Records.

[8] Katie Davis and Beth Clark, *Kisses from Katie: A Story of Relentless Love and Redemption* (New York: Howard Books, 2011), xix–xx.

[9] Jocelyn K. Glei, *Manage Your Day-to-Day: Build Your Routine, Find Your Focus, and Sharpen Your Creative Mind* (Las Vegas, NV: Amazon Publishing, 2013), 91.

[10] Andrew Murray, *Humility* (Minneapolis: Bethany House, 2001), 6.

[11] Hannah Anderson, *Humble Roots: How Humility Grounds and Nourishes Your Soul* (Chicago: Moody Publishers, 2016), 186.

[12]Toni Raiten-D'Antonio, *The Velveteen Principles: A Guide to Becoming Real* (Deerfield Beach, FL: Health Communications, 2007), 24-25.

CHAPTER 8: ENGAGED

[1]Henri J. M. Nouwen, *The Wounded Healer: Ministry in Contemporary Society* (New York: Doubleday, 1979), 72.

[2]Philip Yancey and Paul W. Brand, *The Gift of Pain: Why We Hurt and What We Can Do About It* (Grand Rapids: Zondervan, 1997).

[3]G. Walter Hansen, "The Emotions of Jesus," *Christianity Today*, February 3, 1997, www.christianitytoday.com/ct/1997/february3/7t2042.html.

[4]Ibid.

[5]Timothy Keller, *Walking with God Through Pain and Suffering* (New York: Dutton, 2013), 252-53.

[6]*The Return of the King*, directed by Peter Jackson (New Line Home Entertainment, 2003), DVD.

[7]Christa Wells, "Come Close Now," from the album *Feed Your Soul*, © 2013 Christa Wells, http://christawellsmusic.com/portfolio-view/feed-your-soul-lyrics. Used by permission. Listen on YouTube, www.youtube.com/watch?v=jIYdZPuqjnY.

[8]Christa Wells, email communication to author, July 16, 2014.

[9]"Negative Capability," Keats' Kingdom, 2004–2016, www.keatsian.co.uk/negative-capability.php.

[10]Wells, "Come Close Now."

[11]Brené Brown, *Daring Greatly: How the Courage to Be Vulnerable Transforms the Way We Live, Love, Parent, and Lead* (New York: Gotham Books, 2012), 30.

[12]Charles Duhigg, *The Power of Habit: Why We Do What We Do in Life and Business* (New York: Random House, 2012), 137.

[13]Erin Davis, *Connected: Curing the Pandemic of Everyone Feeling Alone Together* (Nashville, TN: B&H Publishing, 2014), 78.

CHAPTER 9: CAPTIVATED

[1]David Platt, *Radical: Taking Back Your Faith from the American Dream* (Colorado Springs, CO: Multnomah, 2010), 14.

[2]Jason Morehead, "I'm Not So Sure I Want to Live an Epic Life," Opus, November 27, 2014, http://opus.fm/posts/im-not-so-sure-i-want-to-live-an-epic-life.

[3]Timothy Keller, "The Call to Discipleship: Luke 9:20-25, 51-62," *Knowing and Doing*, Winter 2011, C. S. Lewis Institute, www.cslewisinstitute.org /The_Call_to_Discipleship_SinglePage.

[4]Francis Chan and Danae Yankoski, *Forgotten God: Reversing Our Tragic Neglect of the Holy Spirit* (Colorado Springs, CO: David C. Cook, 2009), 92.

[5]Arthur Bennett, ed., *The Valley of Vision: A Collection of Puritan Prayers and Devotions* (Carlisle, PA: Banner of Truth Trust, 1975), 350-51.

[6]Timothy Keller and Katherine Leary Alsdorf, *Every Good Endeavor: Connecting Your Work to God's Work* (New York: Dutton, 2012), 120.

[7]D. L. Mayfield, "Downward Mobility," D. L. Mayfield (personal website), May 27, 2013, http://dlmayfield.wordpress.com/2013/05/27/downward -mobility.

[8]Jen Hatmaker, in "Thursday Is for Thinkers: Jen Hatmaker," *The Exchange: The Blog of Ed Stetzer*, February 9, 2012, www.christianitytoday.com/ edstetzer/2012/february/thursday-is-for-thinkers-jen-hatmaker.html.

[9]*Born into Brothels: Calcutta's Red Light Kids*, by Zana Briski and Ross Kauffman (Red Light Films, 2004).

[10]Kate McCord, *In the Land of Blue Burqas* (Chicago: Moody Publishers, 2012).

[11]"How Would the World Change if Every Girl Was Educated?," Visually, October 2, 2012, http://visual.ly/how-would-world-change-if-every-girl-was-educated.

[12]Ekemini Uwan, "#BlackLoveMatters: A Reminder from an Unexpected Source," Christ and Pop Culture, March 2, 2015, http://christandpopculture .com/blacklovematters-reminder-unexpected-source.

[13]Paul David Tripp, *A Quest for More: Living for Something Bigger Than You* (Greensboro, NC: New Growth Press, 2008), 18.

PARTING WORDS

[1]Credit goes to Laura Karr for encouraging me that I didn't need to be perfect at being uncomfortable in order to write this book.